The Gestures of God

Explorations in Sacramentality

The Gestures of God

Explorations in Sacramentality

Edited by Geoffrey Rowell and
Christine Hall

continuum
LONDON · NEW YORK

Continuum
The Tower Building
11 York Road
London SE1 7NX

15 East 26th Street
New York
NY 10010

www.continuumbooks.com

First published 2004

British Library Cataloguing-in-Publication Data
A catalogue record for this book is available from the British Library.

ISBN 0-8264-7782-8

Typeset by Servis Filmsetting Ltd, Manchester
Printed and bound by MPG Books Ltd, Bodmin, Cornwall

Contents

Contributors' Biographies

Jeremy S. Begbie is Associate Principal of Ridley Hall, Cambridge, and Honorary Professor at the University of St Andrews, where he directs 'Theology through the Arts' at the Institute for Theology, Imagination and the Arts. He teaches systematic theology at Ridley Hall, and in the University of Cambridge. He studied music and philosophy at Edinburgh University, and theology at Aberdeen and Cambridge. A professionally trained musician, he has performed extensively as a pianist, oboist and conductor. He is ordained and has been a member of the Church of England's Doctrine Commission. His publications include *Music in God's Purposes*, *Voicing Creation's Praise* and *Theology, Music and Time*.

Peter C. Bouteneff teaches courses in dogmatic theology, patristics, spirituality and ecumenism at St Vladimir's Orthodox Theological Seminary in the suburbs of New York. He has worked for several years in theological dialogue, chiefly as Executive Secretary for Faith and Order at the World Council of Churches, and has written extensively on Orthodox relations with the WCC. He has recently co-authored with Anna Marie Aagaard *Beyond the East West Divide: The WCC and the 'Orthodox Problem'*. He holds DPhil and MPhil degrees from Oxford, as well as an MDiv from St Vladimir's and a BMus from New England Conservatory of Music, where he studied jazz.

David Brown was born in Scotland. He was educated at the Universities of Edinburgh, Oxford and Cambridge, and was, from 1976 to 1990, a Fellow of Oriel College, Oxford, where he taught philosophical theology and ethics. In 1990 he moved to his present post as Van Mildert Professor of Divinity at the University of Durham, where he is also a Residentiary Canon of the city's cathedral. His books include *Tradition and Imagination* and *Discipleship and Imagination*, which investigated some of the ways in which God continues to speak to his people through a developing, imaginative tradition. More recently, he has published *God and Enchantment of Place*, in which he explores what used to be called natural religion, how experiences of the natural world and built environment can help provide people with a sense of the presence of God. He was elected a Fellow of the British Academy in 2002.

John Drane teaches practical theology at the University of Aberdeen and at Fuller Seminary, California. For more than twenty years, he has been actively involved in ecumenical mission and ministry both in the UK and internationally, and is co-chair of the Mission Theology Advisory Group of the Archbishops' Council of the Church of England and of Churches Together in Britain and Ireland. His work engages with the interface between popular culture and Christian spirituality and he is the author of *The McDonaldization of the Church*, *Biblical Faith and Cultural Change*, and co-author with Olive Fleming Drane of *Family Fortunes: faith-full caring for today's families*.

Crispin H.T. Fletcher-Louis read Theology at Keble College, Oxford, where he also wrote a doctorate thesis on the influence of Jewish angelology on the Christology and soteriology of Luke Acts. Since then he has taught Biblical Studies at King's College, London, and in the Universities of Durham and Nottingham. His second book, *All the Glory of Adam: Liturgical Anthropology and the Dead Sea Scrolls* is an examination of the role of Jewish Temple cosmology in the creation of an experience and pattern of belief that anticipates the Christian doctrine of deification. He is generally interested in the role of the Temple and its symbolism in the better understanding of biblical religion and theology.

Christine Hall is Convenor of the Windsor Consultation on Sacrament and Sacramentality. She was educated at King's College, London, and the School of Slavonic and East European Studies, London. Her initial research was in Romanian Orthodox Theology, and she has contributed to two symposia in sacramental theology, *Confession and Absolution* and *The Oil of Gladness*. She is co-Director of the Anglo-Nordic Diaconal Research Project and a major contributor to its publications: *The Ministry of the Deacon, vol. 1 – Anglican-Lutheran Perspectives* and *vol. 2 – Ecclesiological explorations.*

Timothy Jenkins has been Dean of Jesus College, Cambridge, since 1992, and Assistant Director of Research in the University of Cambridge from 2001. He studied Social Anthropology at Oxford, undertaking fieldwork in both France and England. He was ordained priest in Bristol in 1986, and served as Chaplain to the University of Nottingham from 1988 to 1992. He is author of *Fieldwork in English Everyday Life: an Ethnographic Approach* and a number of articles.

Ann Loades is Emeritus Professor of Divinity, University of Durham, where she was the first woman to hold a personal Chair. She was awarded a CBE in the 2001 New Year's Honours List (the first and so far the only such award for 'services to Theology'). She undertook various responsibilities for the Arts and Humanities Research Board 1999–2003. Her research interests have embraced theodicy in western European thought between the eighteenth and twentieth centuries; theology and the significance of gender; and most recently, sacramental theology and spirituality. She has lectured widely both nationally and internationally, and is the author and co-editor of seventeen books, and many essays and articles.

David N. Power, a native of Dublin, Ireland, is a Roman Catholic Priest and member of the religious community of the Missionary Oblates of Mary Immaculate. He is Emeritus Professor in the School of Theology and Religious Studies at The Catholic University of America, Washington, DC, USA., where he has taught since 1977. Previously he taught theology in Ireland and at The Pontifical Gregorian University, Rome. In recent years he has been a visiting professor at theology institutes in Canada, South Africa and French Polynesia. He is the author of several books in the area of liturgical and sacramental theology, among them *The Eucharistic Mystery*, *Sacrament* and *Word of the Lord*.

Susan A. Ross is Professor of Theology and Faculty Scholar at Loyola University Chicago. She is the author of *Extravagant Affections: A Feminist Sacramental Theology*, the co-editor with Maureen A. Tilley of *Broken and Whole: Essays on Religion and the Body*, and the author of numerous articles and book chapters on sacramental theology, embodiment and sexuality, feminist ethics and liturgy. She served as the Director of the Women's Studies Program at Loyola and has also served on the Boards of the Catholic Theological Society of America, the College Theology Society, and the Society of Christian Ethics. Her current project is on the relationship between feminist theology and ethics and theological aesthetics.

Geoffrey Rowell is Anglican Bishop in Europe and Emeritus Fellow of Keble College, Oxford. He holds the DD of the University of Oxford. His extensive published works include *The Vision Glorious: Themes and Personalities of the Catholic Revival in Anglicanism*, and he was recently a compiler of the symposium *Love's Redeeming Work: the Anglican Quest for Holiness*. He has served on many bodies including the Doctrine and Liturgical Commissions of the Church of England, and is currently co-Chair of the Anglican-Oriental Orthodox Joint Doctrinal Commission and Vice Chair of the Inter-Anglican Standing Commission on Ecumenical Relations.

Jyoti Sahi was born in Pune, India. He studied art at Camberwell School of Arts and Crafts, London, and, returning to India, he worked, from 1963, with Bede Griffiths on the relationship between Indian spirituality and Christian monastic life. Later, moving to Bangalore, he became consultant to the newly founded Centre for the Bible, Catechetics and Liturgy, set up in 1967 by the Catholic Bishops' Conference of India to look at the whole issue of inculturation. He is still associated with this work and has been involved in design for places of worship and on images of meditation, connecting Christian liturgical signs with Hindu and Buddhist symbols. His has written widely in these areas and is the creator of numerous works of art.

Foreword

by Rowan Williams

The belief of Christians is not simply that God created the world, but that, in creating, he made a world that would speak of him: 'the heavens declare the glory of God' says Psalm 19; even in the silence of the material world, God communicates who and what he is. And for those creatures who are given the gifts of speech and imagination, the call and challenge to speak of God is a far richer matter. Human creatures are summoned to relate to the world and to use its resources in such a way that God's self-offering in love comes through; and they are given the power and freedom to do this by the Spirit who unites them to the Word of God in human flesh, Jesus crucified and raised. When we engage in the action of the Eucharist, we show first what Jesus did and does, and then what humanity in Jesus may do: as he makes new meaning out of the bread and wine by his words, so we are enabled to make our world carry the truth of God's sacrificial love. Sacramentality is not a general principle that the world is full of 'sacredness': it is the very specific conviction that the world is full of the life of a God whose nature is known in Christ and the Spirit. The meaning we make in all our creative activity has to be informed by this kind of holiness. We live in a world alive with God, but that life comes to light fully only when seen in connection with 'Christ the Sacrament', to use the words of one modern theologian.

I hope that the papers from this Windsor consultation will not only inform but excite. In a context where we are still confused about how we as believers approach the natural world, they should focus and inspire delight, reverence, expectation.

Every blessing for this enterprise.

Rowan Cantuar,
September 2003

Introduction

by Christine Hall

A Consultation on *Sacrament and Sacramentality* brought twenty-one invited scholars and researchers together for four days in 2003 at St George's House, Windsor Castle. Participants came from Romania, Serbia, the USA, India, Sweden, Finland and Italy, as well as England and Scotland. They were from the Anglican, Roman Catholic, Lutheran, Methodist and Orthodox (Chalcedonian) traditions, with research specialisms in biblical studies, historical, systematic and practical theology, ecclesiology, ecumenism, liturgy, ecclesiastical history, feminist theology, art, music and sociology. The British Academy indicated the academic importance of the exercise by awarding a conference grant; the Confraternity of the Blessed Sacrament recognized the need for the Church to take this exploration seriously and made a very generous contribution, without which the Consultation would not have been possible. St George's House, Windsor, was an ideal location.

The Presidential Address and the ten papers given at the Consultation are all below: we regret that it is not possible to recreate for the reader the virtuoso piano playing with which Jeremy Begbie demonstrated the points in his paper and the examples of his own art with which Jyoti Sahi illustrated his. A number of prior concerns and observations gave impetus to this Consultation, not least among them the fact that sacramental theology, as traditionally conceived, seems to feature less and less on academic teaching and research programmes in many parts of the world. Moreover, the sacramental reality of the Church seems more rarely taken as read, a fact that is observably affecting international ecumenical deliberations, as well as attitudes to leadership and authority in the Church at large. Churches with an overtly sacramental approach are losing adherents, except perhaps in places where Christian communities are under severe pressure and where non-sacramental forms of Christian worship are less readily available as an alternative. At the same time, it is arguable that in many places the Church has withdrawn from large areas of human experience that have previously been its concern,[1] and that those who are leaving it or are not attracted by it are seeking a wide range of alternative 'sacramental' experiences.[2] The very title of the Consultation reflected both the current difficulty in delineating the field, as well as the organizers' intention to explore as widely as possible. There was a concern to lose nothing of the valued insights and practices of the past, whilst asking a series of questions about them: What relevance do they retain? What alternative forms have they already taken? What kind of opposing tendencies have they engendered or do they have to face in the present day?

A decade ago the papers given at such a Consultation in Windsor would no doubt have been very different. The ambient situation – theologically and socially – was different, as indicated, for example, in an article published in 1994 and entitled 'Sacramental Theology: A Review of Literature',[3] one of whose authors presented a paper at Windsor in 2003.[4] In a little more than fifty pages, the authors of this article mapped the landscape of sacramentality as it was then envisaged. Much of what they observed is still the case: for example, the disciplinary complexity and the variety of philosophical methods and theories integrated into the exploration of sacramental theology, or rather theologies. By comparison with 1994, it emerged from the Windsor Consultation that 'sacramental theology' had to a great extent emancipated itself from dogmatics. The disciplinary complexity that might perhaps have been expected to be resolved, at

least to some extent, through liturgical reform and the ecclesiology it reflects, and through liturgical theology as a whole, had
in fact become more complex. This in itself was clearly a field
in which further study was required. At the same time, the
concept of sacramentality had been broadened to an extent that
could not have been envisaged a decade ago. Professor Sven-Erik
Brodd, Dean of the Faculty of Theology, University of Uppsala,
drew attention to this in the review of the Consultation that he
presented to the final plenary session. He noted that nineteenth
and early twentieth century phenomenology of religion had
been brought into the field of sacramental theology in what was,
for him, an unexpected way. He supposed that this was as much
a surprise to the participants in the Consultation, or perhaps it
was taken entirely for granted, since none of the papers had specifically mentioned it. The concept of culture was also central to
deliberations at Windsor, and this, he thought, was an area that
would continue to present problems to all types of sacramental
theology, unless it is given urgent clarification from an academic
perspective.

It would appear that, since 1994, the concepts of 'sacrament'
and 'sacramental theology' have been drifting apart, perhaps not
only because they are distinct from one another but because
theology on the sacraments has hitherto been founded on a too
institutionalized, even poorly developed, ecclesiology, while
'sacramental theology' suggests a broader and more dynamic
field. Some scholars present at Windsor would, however, argue
that its biblical basis has been insufficient. That being said, the
papers offered at the Consultation, as the reader will verify
below, did not emphasize concepts so much as contents, definitions so much as descriptions. The openness with which the
consultation was structured threw up conceptual ambiguities
that might have been disturbing to some viewpoints, though in
fact they were more creative than destructive. However, for the
sake of clarity and mutual understanding, a closer analysis of
ongoing conceptual developments is needed.

In discussion at Windsor, reference was also made to a perceived tension between the incarnational and the eschatological

in sacramental theology. At times, eschatology has been placed over against sacramental theology, especially where sacramental theology has been defined predominantly as incarnational theology. This latter approach was rejected during the Consultation in favour of a sacramental theology that embraces both what is incarnational and what is eschatological in character.

As in some of the remarks above, I am indebted to Sven-Erik Brodd's review for the major part of the following proposals (not placed in order of priority) for further research and enquiry, which formed part of his summing up of the Consultation:

a) A mapping exercise, similar to that undertaken by Duffy, Irwin and Power in 1994, but using the enhanced electronic information technology now available, would make clearer the extent to which the situation is changing;

b) The biblical referents and ecclesiological presuppositions that underpin traditional and emergent concepts of sacramental theology require further identification and exploration;

c) As mentioned above, conceptual ambiguities have arisen and are in need of closer identification and examination;

d) The complexity of philosophical and theological paradigms that continue to govern sacramental theologies that have been transported from their place of origin and contextualized elsewhere requires careful deconstruction;

e) The dialogical character of sacramentality, not only as a relatively new phenomenon, but as an interdisciplinary field already transcending the locus of the theology of the sacraments would repay ongoing discussion.

Participants at Windsor were in favour of a follow-up conference on a larger scale, in about two years' time, and possibilities for this are already being explored. By its nature, sacramentality is essentially communicative and needs to find dialogical expression especially as it is transcending traditional academic and confessional borders of many kinds. At the moment, however, it is on the ecumenical agenda mainly as portrayed by Jean Rigal in his article 'La sacramentalité comme question oecuménique',[5] that is, without the rich variety of connotations explored at Windsor.

Notes

1 See David Brown, pp. 21–36 below.
2 See John Drane, pp. 37–55 below.
3 Regis A. Duffy, Kevin W. Irwin and David N. Power, in *Theological Studies*, 55 (1994), pp. 657–705.
4 See David Power, pp. 145–59 below.
5 In *Nouvelle revue théologique* 124 (2002), pp. 57–78.

1

The significance of sacramentality[1]

Geoffrey Rowell

It is particularly appropriate that a consultation exploring sacraments and sacramentality should have begun its work on Michaelmas Day, the Feast of St Michael and All Angels. The collect for Michaelmas Day in the 1662 Book of Common Prayer speaks of the God who 'created angels and men in a wonderful order'. Immediately we are brought into a sacramental and symbolic universe, which speaks of an ordered hierarchy of being with its foundation in worship, pre-eminently eucharistic worship, in which almost universally the prayers of the Church are joined with those of 'angels and archangels and all the company of heaven'. The vision of Isaiah in the Temple at the moment of his call is the source of the *Sanctus*, the *Holy, holy, holy, Lord God of Sabaoth* of the angelic armies of heaven, which occurs again, of course, in the Book of Revelation. As Cyril of Jerusalem reminds us in his Catechetical Lectures, 'the reason of our reciting this confession of God, delivered down to us from the Seraphim, is this, that so we may be partakers with the hosts of the world above in their Hymn of praise'.[2] This sense of Christian worship as being a participation in the worship of heaven, and of the angels as enabling that participation, is powerfully maintained in the Ethiopian Orthodox Church, where the angels guard with their swords the entrance to the sanctuary,

1

and look down with many eyes on the human worshippers from many painted ceilings. In 1974, when I took an Oxford University Expedition to the highlands of Tigray, looking for rock churches and ancient manuscripts, we came at one point in our expedition to the Church of Yohannes Metmek, Gazien – the Church of John the Baptist, situated on the precipitous edge of the Rift Valley. It was the feast day of the church and crowds had gathered for the Liturgy, but a storm and a flash flood the night before had made us late and we arrived almost at the end of the Liturgy. We asked if we might see the church but were told that we must wait for the holiness to wear off. The angels had descended for the Liturgy and they had now returned to heaven (some Ethiopians will tell you that the dismissal at the end of the Liturgy is addressed to the angels, not to the earthly congregation). We had to wait almost three hours before it was thought 'safe' for us to enter. Ethiopian Christianity, with its strong Jewish elements, is a window into an ancient sacramental world. Every church is consecrated by the presence of the *tabot* or Ark, and each *Timkat*, the feast of the Baptism of the Lord, the *tabots* are carried, wrapped in ornate cloths, to lie beside water overnight – a rite with cross-cultural parallels in the annual washing of the Buddha statues in the Pak Ou caves north of the great cluster of temples in Luang Prabang in Laos. Ethiopian churches have elaborate schemes of wall-painting, but these are generally covered with veils. The saints and angels are present, but their representations may need to be veiled. The forms of the churches, be they rectangular or circular, gradually move from the outer walls, where prayer can take place by a circling of the church building, just as in the Buddhist monasteries of Bhutan, to the inner ambulatory, and finally to the sanctuary, the holy of holies which only the clergy can enter. An Ethiopian festival can assemble crowds of worshippers outside the church, with only the clergy inside. In other Eastern traditions – the Armenian and Syriac, for example – the drawing of the veil at particular moments in the Eucharist creates a sacred drama in which there is movement between heaven and earth – the sacramental coming of the Lord and the Lord coming forth from his sanctuary, so that the worshippers may be caught into heaven. There are deep roots here with Jewish Temple liturgy, the significance of which has been recently underlined in the work of Margaret Barker.[3]

Not only are the church buildings of Ethiopia sacramental but so also is the Ethiopian elaboration of the cross in both processional and blessing crosses, the cross being 'the seal of Christ and of the Trinity'. It is the healing sign of the triumph of sacrificial love. In the interlacing patterns of many Ethiopian crosses, the cross as the tree of life can find the birds nesting in its branches.[4] The cross can also be used as a symbol that incorporates basic Christian teaching as does my own pectoral cross (a copy of a fifteenth-century Ethiopian blessing cross), which has the four arms like rams' heads (Jesus the sacrificial Lamb of God), with the spaces in between as the four hearts of the four Gospels testifying to the love of God; each arm surmounted with a trefoil of the Trinity, and the four trefoils on each of the four arms representing the twelve apostles. On the back are decorations – 'but, no', said an Ethiopian priest who read my cross for me, 'the twenty-four elders around the throne'. The cross in this Christian culture functions like the Western medieval memory systems.[5] Here is indeed a symbolic universe, a universe which has the cross imprinted on it, that cosmic cross of which Justin Martyr spoke when he made reference to Plato saying in the *Timaeus* that the *Logos* was set like a *Tau* in the heavens.[6]

Despite the stern Islamic repudiation of images, carpets can have sacramental significance, with the niche and lamp for a holy place for prayer, and with the rich and elaborate representations of paradise gardens. As Volkmar Gantzhorn has argued there is much in the rich traditions of Middle Eastern carpet design which is drawn from a pattern of Christian symbolism, particularly the cross.[7] When wealthy Europeans or Americans buy oriental carpets and put them on their floors or on their walls they are in effect bringing a portion of paradise into their houses. They might even be said to be doing something sacramental.

The sacramental and the incarnational are of course closely linked. It was at the root of John of Damascus' defence of icons in the eighth century. The reality of the Incarnation is testified to by Scripture, and no less by the icons that depict that Incarnation. John, whose opponents attacked him as 'Mansur the Saracen-minded', wrote that:

> when we have not the Lord's passion in mind and see the image of Christ's crucifixion, his saving passion is brought to remembrance, and we fall down and worship not the material but that which is imaged: just as we do not worship the material of which the Gospels were made, nor the material of the Cross, but that which they typify . . . It is just the same also in the case of the Mother of the Lord. For the honour which we give to her is referred to him who was made of her incarnate.[8]

In the same section of *De Fide Orthodoxa*, John argues powerfully that 'since God has appeared in the flesh and has interacted with man, I am able to depict the visible aspect of God. I do not worship matter; I worship the creator of matter, who for my sake became matter himself'. Matter was 'instrumental in my salvation, and for this reason is endowed with divine power and grace'. In another treatise, he writes:

> The wood of the cross . . . is it not indeed matter? . . . The gold and silver used to make crosses, patens, chalices, are they not matter? And is not before everything else the Lord's Body and Blood matter? . . . Do not despise matter! It is not without honour . . . I honour material things, not as though they were God, but inasmuch as they are replete with divine energy and grace.[9]

As Cardinal Christoph Schönborn comments, for Christians 'matter does not lie in the farthest and lowest relationship to God, as Neo-Platonism holds . . . on the contrary: the entire economy of salvation has always employed material things too. Thus matter is not at all an obstacle on the way to God, but becomes by its participation in Christ's mystery the medium through which salvation is accomplished.'[10] Thus grounded in the Incarnation, matter matters, and sacraments and the sacramental. Our human senses and materiality and bodiliness are not things to be escaped from and left behind, but to be transformed and transfigured. The *soma pneumatikon*, the spiritual body, of which Paul speaks in 1 Corinthians, is not the ectoplasm of nineteenth-century spiritualists. It does not mean 'a body consisting of spirit' but 'a body animated by the Holy Spirit', as the Doctrine Commission of the Church of England makes clear.

The only clue we have to this bodily reality is the glorified body of the Risen Lord, for the resurrection of Jesus is the seminal event of the new creation. In his victory over death the Last Day has arrived. The resurrection of Jesus is the beginning within history of a process whose fulfilment lies beyond history, in which the destiny of humanity and the destiny of the universe are together to find their fulfilment in a liberation from decay and futility.[11]

It is to this eschatological future that the Church looks in hope and anticipation. In the Eucharist we 'proclaim the Lord's death until he comes' (1 Corinthians 11.26), sharing now in the bread of the day of the Lord that we may be made the Lord's body and transformed into his likeness, commanded in St Augustine's words to 'be what we receive and receive what we are'.[12] In this context the aphorism of Ludwig Feuerbach, the nineteenth-century materialist philosopher, has, as Fr Alexander Schmemann pointed out – ironically – a deep and true meaning: 'Man is what he eats'.[13]

A century earlier than John of Damascus, Maximus the Confessor in his *Mystagogia* had written of the church building and the liturgy celebrated within it. Every Christian, he writes, 'should visit the holy church of God often' and should

never miss the holy liturgy performed in it, both because of the holy angels who are in attendance and always take notice of those who come, bringing them to God's attention and interceding for them, and because of the grace of the Holy Spirit, which is always present in an invisible way but is most especially so during the time of the holy liturgy. This grace enfolds all those who attend, creates them anew, and truly leads each of them, according to his own capacities, to a more divine way of living; it brings each one closer to what the sacred mysteries signify, even when the individual does not experience this consciously.[14]

For Maximus, as von Balthasar points out, 'world and liturgy share a christological foundation' and the eucharistic action records the whole providential history of God's salvation.[15] As von Balthasar again emphasizes, for Maximus 'the mystery of supernatural life, far from being thrown over the world as something foreign and purely "historical", is rather something that involves and transforms all natural being down to its deepest foundations . . . the law of Christ, despite its historical character, is a cosmological law.' The transfiguring experience into which Christians are drawn is a participation in the total incarnational reality of the Christ who emptied himself, made himself nothing, drained himself in the utter self-giving of love. As a seventeenth-century English divine, Mark Frank, put it in a Christmas sermon:

> Of his emptiness to-day it is, that we have all received, that we still receive all: there is nothing we receive, but it is from this day's emptiness; and there is nothing that we receive not from it, from his this day's emptying himself into the form of a servant, from this day's exanition . . . His thus very emptying himself for us, his thus very emptying himself upon us, is the very fulness of his grace and favour to us: the day, then, wherein it was, a day of fulness, where he was full, and we were filled; he full of grace and we filled from it.[16]

Frank's sense of the Incarnation as the mystery which is both God's self-emptying and the fullness of the grace of God's self-giving is at one with Maximus' affirmation that

> the mystery of the Incarnation of the Word contains in itself the force and meaning of all the challenging puzzles and symbols of Scripture, as well as the significant content of all visible and intelligible creatures. Whoever understands the mystery of the Cross and the grave has grasped the essential content (λογος) of all the things we have mentioned; and whoever, in addition, has been initiated into the mysterious meaning and power of the Resurrection knows the primordial (προηγουμενως) purpose for which God created the universe.[17]

The sacramental life of the Church into which Christians are plunged at their Baptism is cosmic in its dimension. Christ is the one who fills all things, the one through whom all things are created, and 'from his fullness we have, all of us, received . . .' (John 1.16). The sacramental expression of that saving and trans-figuring reality, whether it be in 'the sacraments' narrowly so defined, or in the setting forth of this vision in buildings, art and liturgy, calls us to a contemplative awareness, a transformation of our imaginations, which are, in one sense, because we are made in the image of God with the potential to grow into his likeness which is Christ, already fundamentally orientated or open to such an awareness. The life of faith is a commitment of our whole being, and the grace which sustains is the energy of the Spirit transforming us into the likeness of Christ, whose very character and being is sacrificial love. So the contemplation to which we are called can never remain at the level of aesthetic enjoyment but always involves an *ascesis*. The sacrament of the Eucharist is indeed a feeding on Christ, in which, in the striking words of the Anglican-Roman Catholic International Commission (ARCIC) agreed statement on the Eucharist, we 'enter into the movement of his self-offering'.[18] The life of prayer can be, as the great Spanish Carmelites, St Teresa of Avila and St John of the Cross so often remind us, a stripping away of the very images and symbols, which are sacramental in their character and which have been the door-ways to life in Christ. The kataphatic, the way of the affirmation of images, must always have as its counterpart the apophatic, which speaks of the failure of human language, whether expressed in word or sacrament, those two earthen vessels that only point to a reality which transcends them. Worship as adoration knows both the Lord who comes to us in the simplest things, in the bread and wine of the Eucharist, and yet draws us into a mystery of love which no words or symbols can contain. It is not surprising, rather absolutely required, that the Christian tradition which has engen-dered so much richness of art and beauty in painting, architecture, music and poetry, has also had those who have been iconoclasts, tearing down images which are thought to supplant the God who cannot be represented, and in so supplanting distort. Yet the sim-plicity and silence of the Quaker meeting house is in its own way a sacrament of divine presence, that presence, of which the Welsh

THE GESTURES OF GOD

poet-priest, R. S. Thomas, wrote that 'its absence was as its presence',[19] echoing perhaps Elijah on Horeb where God was encountered not in the dramatic phenomena of earthquake, wind and fire, but in the 'sound of thin silence'.[20] Words indeed, as the poet T. S. Eliot wrote in *Burnt Norton*,

> ....strain,
> Crack and sometimes break under the burden,
> Under the tension, slip, slide perish,
> Decay with imprecision, will not stay in place,
> Will not stay still.[21]

Mythologizing and demythologizing are perhaps a necessarily alternating rhythm embedded in the sheer fact of the inadequacy of our human language to speak of what of necessity lies beyond it. John Bowker reminds us at the end of his investigation of the religious imagination and the sense of God:

> All types and shadows have their ending, and any characterization of theistic reality is necessarily inadequate, since it is derivative, not from an immediate vision, but from a direct intuition. The strong insistence on the *via negativa*, on the *bila kaif*, on the *neti neti*, not this, not this, of all developed theistic traditions makes the same point. Yet tentative approximations are possible, because the inputs from the claimed reality are not themselves without character. They impress themselves on the human subject . . . as though they are signals transmitted either directly in the mode of contemplation or meditation, or through the channels of occurrence in the natural order, through, for example, observing the external world in a particular way, or through the encounter with another person, or through the rituals and symbols of particular religious contexts.[22]

In Western Christendom, the Reformation division had an enormous impact on sacramental theology. Although the Reformation was not everywhere iconoclastic; for example in the Scandinavian countries and in Lutheran confessions which allowed many things as *adiaphora*, nevertheless the more radical Reformed tradition held that only things explicitly commanded in Scripture might legitimately be used as aids to devotion –

hence the Puritan disputes in England about the use of the ring in marriage, and issues about vestments which even now can cause dissension amongst Anglicans. Protestants, repudiating the sacrifice of the Mass, sought to encourage the reception of Communion. Archbishop Cranmer attacked the late medieval practice of non-communicating attendance. The faithful went, he said, to look on an external miracle, defined as transubstantiation, but Christ ordained the Eucharist in order that he might be transubstantiate in us, as is so well expressed in his Prayer of Humble Access, 'that we may evermore dwell in him and he in us'. Perhaps this also lies behind Cranmer's dismemberment of the traditional canon, so that Communion is received immediately after the words of institution and the prayer of oblation is made by worshippers now united with the indwelling Christ. The abolition of the Mass, the use of vernacular language for worship, did not necessarily mean a repudiation of Christ's presence in the Eucharist, though, as we know, there were fierce debates as to how this might be, with the Swiss Reformer, Zwingli, on the far left reducing the elements to mere memorial signs. For Calvin we are taken up to heaven *oculis animisque* ('by our eyes and minds'). He is emphatic that we do not drag Christ down from heaven, except by outward symbol and the Spirit, though feeding on the body is not a 'purely mental or cognitive operation'.[23] He admits that the Eucharist is a mystery 'too sublime for my intelligence to grasp or my words to declare'.

> Here, then, without any arguing, I embrace the truth of God in which I may safely rest content. Christ proclaims that his flesh is the food, his blood the drink of my soul. I offer him my soul to be fed with such food. In his sacred supper he bids me take, eat, and drink his body and blood under the symbols of bread and wine: I have no doubt that he truly proffers them and that I receive them.[24]

Recent revisionist studies of the English Reformation have argued for the vitality of Catholicism on the eve of the Reformation, and have suggested that the Protestant agenda, in the destruction of the shrines of saints and places of pilgrimage, was far from welcome. A Devon convert to Protestantism on the other hand, declaring that the true Church only existed 'where the true faith and confidence in Christ's death and passion, and his only merits and deservings are extolled and our own depressed', maintained that the Eucharist was only commemorative rather than miraculous.[25] Maybe there are just the beginnings here of the sidelining of the sacramental. For it may be argued that the seeds of later rationalism were sown in Protestant arguments about such things as the mode of the presence of Christ in the sacrament, and perhaps rooted further back in the logical disputation of scholasticism and the divergence between monastic and university theology.

These are complex arguments, yet there is little doubt that the background to Enlightenment deism was often in a Protestant context, where there were tensions between the rationalist dogmatic theology of Protestant scholasticism and the subjective devotion of the various pietist movements. When the poet Samuel Taylor Coleridge encountered German philosophy and early debates about biblical criticism, he saw both the importance of the role of the imagination in Christian reflection and the weakness of rationalist, deductive theologizing. 'The almighty goodness', he wrote, 'does not dwell in generalities, nor abide in abstractions', and his concern for image and symbol, both in his poetry and in his religious and philosophical writing, was a powerful influence on the religious thought of nineteenth-century England. There is continuity here with many of the concerns of the Oxford Movement, that movement of Catholic Revival in the Church of England, which had at its heart the rediscovery of the importance of the sacramental. Even if it often wore a neo-Gothic and medieval dress, at its heart it was more than mere antiquarianism. It is no accident that John Keble and, to a lesser extent, John Henry Newman were poets, with a deep concern for the power of language. In his *Lectures on Poetry*, delivered in Oxford in Latin, as was then customary, Keble speaks of the 'healing power of poetry'.[26] It is a vehicle for catharsis, 'a channel through which emotion finds expression, and that a safe, regulated expression'. In other words its imaginative character has a deep and close affinity with spiritual life and growth. Newman speaks of the very being of the Church as poetry, its sacramental order as disciplining raw religious enthusiasm. The same Spirit who sweeps over the waters of chaos at creation orders the sacramental life of the Church. Keble links closely poets and prophets, and Newman, writing on tradition in the Church as the living, shaping presence of the Spirit, calls prophetic tradition the pattern of liturgy, prayer and sacramental worship, which is the vehicle of the faith and is only as necessity demands expressed formally in creeds and conciliar decisions. Poetry, writes Keble, as he comes to the final lecture in which he discusses the relation of poetry and theology, 'lends Religion her wealth of symbols and similes; Religion restores these again to Poetry, clothed with so splendid a radiance that they appear to be no longer merely symbols, but to partake, I might almost say, of the nature of sacraments'.[27] In his religious poetry Keble draws both on the natural order, the 'book' of creation or nature, and the symbolic pattern of the Bible drawn out in Church tradition, particularly in the sanctification of time through the Church's year, and the theology of type and anti-type, in which meaning is conveyed through Old Testament stories illuminating and being seen as brought to fulfilment in the New Testament. Newman much admired the series of lectures on *Types and Prophecies*, which Edward Bouverie Pusey delivered in 1836. He wrote to Pusey in 1839 that he believed that this exposition of the Christian imagination was the only way to combat the scepticism of Strauss's *Life of Jesus*.[28] So Pusey writes:

> The inherent significance of images receives its full direction and completeness in God's revelation. In heathenism and in the natural world they are significant, but not of necessity, prophetic. They express truth, but give no earnest that it shall be realised, unless indeed in so far as we may
>> See in heaven and earth
>> In all fair things around
>> Strong yearnings for a blest new birth
>> With sinless glories crowned.[29]

11

Pusey is, of course, quoting from Keble's poem for Septuagesima Sunday, in *The Christian Year*. This poem is Keble's most extensive poetic exposition of the sacramental character of the natural world, created by God and seen through Christian eyes. Pusey himself, learned in Hebrew and Syriac, familiar with the writings of that much earlier poetic theologian, St Ephraem, and alert to the contemporary challenges of German theology, was convinced that sacramentalism, so deeply rooted in the Scriptures and the Fathers, was in urgent need of recovery for the wellbeing of the Church. 'God has appointed', he writes, 'a sort of sacramental union between the type and the archetype, so that the type were nothing except in so far as it represents, and is the medium of conveying the archetype to the mind except thro' the type.' He goes on, with reference to the Eucharist in particular:

> The pseudo-spiritualist and the carnal man alike see in the water, the bread or the wine nothing but the bare element, and thereby each alike deprives himself of the benefits intended for him; the carnal would live on the bread alone, the pseudo-spiritualist without it; the carnal mistakes the clouds and darkness for Him who is enshrined within it, the pseudo-spiritualist would behold Him, who 'men cannot see and live', the light inapproachable 'who no man hath seen or can see': the carnal neglects the revelation, the pseudo-spiritualist would know the unrevealed God . . . The whole system of religion, contemplative and practical, is one of God's condescension: God cometh down to us, not we mount up to God. Its corner-stone and characteristic is 'God manifest in the flesh'. And with this, as God has appointed it, all is in keeping. Neither the letter without the Spirit, nor yet the Spirit without the letter – prayers, which God cometh into the midst of us to hear; earthly Sacraments, yet full of Heaven; earthly words, yet full of the Lord, λογοι proceeding from and setting forth the Λογος. And we, as we walk still by faith and not by sight, must be content to see still the reflected light, 'as in a glass darkly', not 'face to face'.[30]

As Allchin comments, 'thus the images of the Old Testament, no less than the sacraments of the New, are in an indispensable element in our apprehension of the Son of God who has become incarnate, who speaks not to our minds alone, but also to our wills, affections, consciences, imaginations'. It is a grievous mistake to reduce the whole economy of God's revelation to conceptual terms.[31] It is not for nothing that Newman reminded the Evangelical Sir James Stephen that 'Christians receive the Gospel literally on their knees, and in a temper altogether different from that critical and argumentative spirit which sitting and listening engender'.[32] The sacramental concerns of the Oxford Movement Fathers, rooted, as they were, in the doctrines of creation and Incarnation, are but one English example of the recognition of the centrality of sacramentality and of the Christian truth it transmits and effects. Yet, for all the renewal of liturgy in the Churches of the West, there is a concern that the awareness of the sacramental is diminishing. It is part, but only part, of what people may mean in speaking of secularization, itself a highly complex term. René Guénon, in his book *Fundamental Symbols: The Universal Language of Sacred Science*,[33] laments that 'religion is for most people only an affair of sentiment, without any intellectual import. Religion is confused with vague religiosity, or is reduced to a morality. The function of doctrine is reduced as much as possible'.[34] A more recent trenchant expression of concern is Philip J. Lee's *Against the Protestant Gnostics*,[35] which has a particular concern for the anti-sacramental trends in American Protestantism and their consequences. Lee suggests that the early American Puritans, with their Reformed theology, argued like this:

> Because God is sovereign, He has no obligation to use the sacraments. If God wishes to cleanse us by other means than baptism, He can. If He chooses to nourish us by other means than by Holy Communion, He certainly can. They began to infer from this premise that God does *not* choose such means to save us, and because God is not bound to employ the Church itself to do His work, the Church does not occupy an essential role in redemption.[36]

Lee quotes Max Weber's astringent comment on the consequences of later Calvinism – 'the complete elimination of salvation through the Church and the sacraments'.[37] The American

Transcendentalists protested against a graceless, anti-sacramental Church and spawned a liberal syncretism, and fundamentalists reacted against such syncretistically hospitable liberalism. American Protestantism, Lee argues, has to a great degree become desacramentalized, and grape juice served in individual cups undercuts the givenness of the sacramental elements and the unity symbolized by the one chalice. Under the religious legacy of the Masonic Deism of the founding fathers, non-sacramental religion, be it services of the word and no sacraments, or one form or another of liberal syncretism, can characterize much of American Protestantism and what it exports more widely. The indignation of Orthodox Church leaders so recently liberated from Marxist Communism at the proliferation of American missionaries concerned (as they see it) to bring the faith for the first time to Russia and Eastern Europe, can readily be understood. For in the Orthodox world it has been the deeply-rooted pattern of sacramental worship that has maintained the faith under atheist oppression. So Lee comments, quoting Paul Lehmann, on the centrality of the Eucharist to the very being of the Church:

> 'The *koinonia* is either a eucharistic achievement or a conjurer's trick'. Without the particularity of the meal and without the particular Host who presides at the meal, the Church's agenda becomes something quite different from that assigned to it in the New Testament, through the traditions of the Fathers, or even by the Protestant Reformers. The Church without sacraments exists for the purpose of accomplishing certain self-imposed goals which have at best only a tangential connection with the Gospel.[38]

It is the same message found in the poem, *The Incarnate One*, by Edwin Muir, who came to a sacramental and incarnational faith after rejecting the bloodless and oppressive Christianity of his Orkney childhood.

> The windless northern surge, the sea-gull's scream
> And Calvin's kirk crowning the barren brae.
> I think of Giotto the Tuscan shepherd's dream,

14

Christ, man and creature in their inner day.
How could our race betray
The Image, and the Incarnate One unmake
Who chose this form and fashion for our sake?

The Word made flesh here is made word again,
A word made word in flourish and arrogant crook.
See there King Calvin with his iron pen,
And God three angry letters in a book,
And there the logical hook
On which the Mystery is impaled and bent
Into an ideological instrument.[39]

And Muir goes on to warn that 'the fleshless word, growing, will bring us down'.

The sacramental is surely important, and the renewal of sacramental self-understanding is vital for the well-being of the Church. The Christian imagination, and the awareness of its history and development, is of primary concern if we would communicate the faith and find ourselves in worship. 'The image has touched the depths before it stirs the surface' wrote Gaston Bachelard, the French scientist-philosopher-poet.[40] They were words which the remarkable Christian psychotherapist, Dr Murray Cox, believed encapsulated the therapeutic power of image and symbol that inhabits all creative writing, in Shakespeare but above all the Bible.[41] Our world is not devoid of sacramental awareness. When I contributed to a book on the sacrament of anointing, there was an interesting chapter on how the Christian sacramental language of anointing had been taken over by the beauty industry.[42] And when I asked a class of teenagers shortly after the tragic death of Princess Diana what they thought was the meaning of the piles of teddy-bears left alongside the cellophane-wrapped flowers as a memorial, they replied that if it was a new teddy-bear that meant you had given something by spending money on it; if it was one of your old and favourite ones that showed your love by the fact that you were willing to give it up. There is surely just a hint of sacrifice and sacrament there? The late Dr John Coulson in a fascinating and intriguing book, *Religion and Imagination: 'in aid of a grammar of assent'* wrote, following Maurice de la Taille, of Christians as those who put themselves in the order of signs.

Christians are those who separate themselves from the world by speaking and responding in a common language. It is formed (and re-formed) by the liturgy – 'the table of God's word' – nourished by scripture (and therefore analogical), and completed in the living out of what it enjoins. Theologically, it is a language which appeals *through* imagination, *with* reason, *to* the conscience. Poetically, it is resolved in Yeats's questions, thus:

> How but in custom and in ceremony
> Are innocence and beauty born?[43]

But custom and ceremony, word and sacrament, icon, symphony and cantata, are all for the Christian rooted in that one sacrament of the Christ who gives himself into the world, which proclaims the glory of God because it was made through him, to bring about a new creation, a new order that will find its end and goal in the communion of the love of God. It is a vision summed up by Dante in his *Paradiso*, speaking of that worship of heaven, of which in the worship of the Church in Christ we already have a foretaste.

In form then of a pure white rose the saintly host was shown to me, which with His own blood Christ made His bride. But the other bride – who, as it flies, sees and sings His glory who enamours it, and the goodness which made it so great – like a swarm of bees which one moment enflower themselves, and the next return to where their work acquires savour – was descending into the great flower which is adorned with so many petals, and thence reascending to where its love abides for ever. They had their faces all of living flame, and their wings of gold, and the rest so white that no snow reaches such a limit. When they descended into the flower they proffered of the peace and the ardor which they had acquired as they fanned their sides. Nor did the interposing of so great a flying plenitude, between what was above and the flower, impede the vision or the splendour; for the divine light so penetrates through the universe, in measure of its worthiness, that naught can be an obstacle to it. This secure and joyful kingdom, thronged with ancient and with modern folk, had look and love all directed on one mark . . . So, taking my eyes upwards through the living light, I led my eyes along the ranks, now up, now down, and now circling about. I saw faces all given to love, adorned by the light of Another, and by their own smile and movements graced with every dignity.[44]

Not only the angelic host, but, as John Keble would have put it, 'the Saviour in his people crowned'.

Notes

1 Presidential Address to the Consultation on Sacrament and Sacramentality held at St George's House, Windsor Castle, 29 September to 2 October 2003.

2 Cyril of Jerusalem, 'On the Sacred Liturgy and Communion', Lecture XXIII (on the Mysteries, V), *Catechetical Lectures*, in P. Schaff and H. Wace (eds), *The Nicene and Post-Nicene Fathers, vol. VII* (Edinburgh: T&T Clark and Grand Rapids: Eerdmans, repr. 1989), sect. 6, p. 154.

3 Cf. especially Margaret Barker, *The Great High Priest: The Temple Roots of Christian Liturgy* (London & New York: Continuum, 2003); *On Earth as It Is in Heaven: Temple Symbolism in the New Testament* (Edinburgh: T&T Clark, 1995); *The Gate of Heaven: The History and Symbolism of the Temple in Jerusalem* (London: SPCK, 1991).

4 On the symbolic significance of the cross in Ethiopia and its healing power cf. Jacques Mercier, *Art that Heals: Image as Medicine in Ethiopia* (New York: Prestel, 1997), pp. 64–72.

5 Cf. Frances Yates, *The Art of Memory* (Chicago: University of Chicago Press, 1974); Mary Carruthers, *The Craft of Thought: Meditation, Rhetoric and the Making of Images, 400–1200* (Cambridge: Cambridge University Press, 1998).

6 Justin Martyr, *Apology* I, lx.

7 Volkmar Gantzhorn, *The Oriental Christian Carpet: A Presentation of its Development Iconologically and Iconographically from its Beginnings to the 18th Century* (Cologne: Benedikt Taschen Verlag, 1991).

8 John of Damascus, *De Fide Orthodoxa*, xvi.

9 John of Damascus, *Contra imaginum calumniatores, orationes tres*, PG.

94 I.16 (1245AC), II.14 (1300 C), in Christoph Schönborn, *God's Human Face: the Christ-Icon* (San Francisco: Ignatius Press, 1994), pp. 195–6.

10 Schönborn, *God's Human Face*, p. 196.

11 The Doctrine Commission of the Church of England, *The Mystery of Salvation: The Story of God's Gift* (London: Church House Publishing, 1995), pp. 191–2.

12 Cf. Geoffrey Wainwright, *Eucharist and Eschatology* (Oxford: Oxford University Press, 1981).

13 Alexander Schmemann, *World as Sacrament* (London: Darton, Longman and Todd, 1966), p. 10, quoting L. Feuerbach, 'Advertisement to Moleschott', *Lehre der Nahungsmittel: Für das Volk*, (1850), 'Der Mensch ist was er isst'.

14 *Mystagogia* 24; PG 91,701d–704a, in Hans Urs von Balthasar, *Cosmic Liturgy: The Universe according to Maximus the Confessor*, English trans. (San Francisco: Ignatius Press, 2003), p. 318.

15 von Balthasar, *Cosmic Liturgy*, pp. 322–3.

16 Mark Frank, 'The Third Sermon on Christmas-Day', from *LI Sermons Preached by the Reverend Dr Mark Frank* (London, 1672) reprinted in Mark Frank, *Sermons, I* (Library of Anglo-Catholic Theology, Oxford: John Henry Parker, 1849), p. 93.

17 Maximus, *Centuries of Knowledge*, 1, 66; PG 90, 1108AB, in von Balthasar, *Cosmic Liturgy*, p. 278.

18 Statement on Eucharistic Doctrine (1971), in ARCIC *The Final Report* (CTS/SPCK, 1982), sect. 'The Eucharist and the Sacrifice of Christ', para. 5, on p.14.

19 R. S. Thomas, 'Sea-watching' in *Laboratories of the Spirit* (London: Macmillan, 1975), p. 74.

20 Cf. Stephen Prickett, *Words and the Word: Language, Poetics and Biblical Interpretation* (Cambridge: Cambridge University Press, 1986), pp. 7ff.

21 T. S. Eliot, *Four Quartets*, 'Burnt Norton', V.ll. 149–53 (London: Faber & Faber, 1944).

22 John Bowker, *The Religious Imagination and the Sense of God* (Oxford: Oxford University Press, 1978), p. 312.

23 B. A. Gerrish, *Grace and Gratitude: The Eucharistic Theology of John Calvin* (Edinburgh: T&T Clark, 1993), p. 175.

24 An addition to Calvin's *Institutes* in 1543, in Gerrish, *Grace and Gratitude,* p. 174.

25 Robert Whiting, *The Blind Devotion of the People: Popular Religion and The English Reformation* (Cambridge: Cambridge University Press, 1989), p. 153.

26 In much of this section I draw on my lecture on 'John Keble, a Speaking Life – III Poet', delivered at Nashotah House, Wisconsin, USA, in 1992 to mark the bi-centenary of John Keble's birth. This was published together with two other studies of Keble as Priest and Pastor in Charles R. Henery (ed.), *A Speaking Life: the Legacy of John Keble* (Leominster: Gracewing, 1995), pp. 42–66.

27 John Keble, *Lectures on Poetry, 1832–1841,* trans. E. K. Chambers (Oxford: Clarendon Press, 1912), II, p. 481.

28 G. Tracey (ed.), *The Letters and Diaries of John Henry Newman, VII* (Oxford: Clarendon Press, 1995), p. 145.

29 Quoted, from the unpublished manuscript, by A. M. Allchin, in John Coulson and A. M. Allchin, *The Rediscovery of Newman: an Oxford Symposium* (London: Sheed & Ward/SPCK, 1967), p. 66.

30 See Coulson and Allchin, *The Rediscovery of Newman,* pp. 69–70.

31 Ibid., p. 70.

32 John Henry Newman to Sir James Stephen, 16 March 1835, in T. Gornall (ed.), *Letters and Diaries of John Henry Newman, V,* p. 46.

33 R. Guénon, *Symboles fondamentaux de la Science Sacrée* (Éditions Gallimard, 1962); English trans., Martin Lings (ed.), *Fundamental Symbols: The Universal Language of Sacred Science* (Bartlow, Cambridge: Quinta Essentia, 1995).

34 Guénon, *Fundamental Symbols,* p. 4.

35 Philip J. Lee, *Against the Protestant Gnostics* (New York and London: Oxford University Press, 1987).

36 Ibid., p. 177.

37 Max Weber, *The Protestant Ethic and the Spirit of Capitalism* (London: Routledge, 1985), pp. 104–5, quoted in Lee, *Against the Protestant Gnostics,* p. 178.

38 Lee, *Against the Protestant Gnostics,* p. 184, quoting P. Lehmann, *Ethics in a Christian Context* (New York: Harper & Row, 1963), p. 65.

39 Edwin Muir, *Collected Poems* (London: Faber & Faber, 1960), p. 228.

40 G. Bachelard, introduction to *The Poetics of Space* (English trans. Boston: Beacon Press, 1969), quoted in Murray Cox and Alice Theilgaard, *Mutative Metaphors in Psychotherapy: The Aeolian Mode* (London & New York: Tavistock Publications, 1987), p. xiii.

41 Cf. Murray Cox, *Shakespeare as Prompter: The Amending Imagination and The Therapeutic Process* (London: Jessica Kingsley Publications, 1994).

42 Rebecca Abrams and Hugo Slim, 'The Revival of Oils in Contemporary Culture: Implications for the Sacrament of Anointing', in Martin Dudley and Geoffrey Rowell (eds), *The Oil of Gladness: Anointing in the Christian Tradition* (London: SPCK and Collegeville: Liturgical Press, 1993), pp. 169–75.

43 John Coulson, *Religion and Imagination: 'in aid of a grammar of assent'* (Oxford: Clarendon Press, 1981), p. 162. W. B. Yeats' poem is entitled, *Prayer for my daughter.*

44 Dante, *Paradiso,* Canto XXX1 (trans. Charles Singleton) cited in John Pope Hennessy, *Paradiso: The Illuminations to Dante's Divine Comedy by Giovanni di Paolo* (London: Thames & Hudson, 1993), p. 221. Dante's amazing vision in the *Paradiso* found in Giovanni di Paolo an illustrator of exceptional visionary quality whose illuminations, as Pope Hennessy makes clear, are the visual counterpart for those who would follow Dante's journey.

2

Re-conceiving the sacramental

David Brown

Valuing the useless

In talking of the need to re-conceive the sacramental I want to stake out my claim that the Church and its theologians have made a very serious error in withdrawing from theological engagement with large areas of experience that were once the Church's concern. Topics like body and food, music and dance, landscape art and town planning, architecture and gardening were all once integral to a religious conception of the world, whereas, if they are discussed in theological context at all these days, the tendency is to treat them as merely illustrative of questions more appropriately raised elsewhere rather than as raising issues and challenges in their own right.[1] The result is that both in its practice and in its theology Christianity has become a very inward looking religion with its perceived external relevance almost wholly confined to ethics and politics. It is partly in the hope of reversing that trend that I have embarked on two large volumes entitled *God and Enchantment of Place* and *God and Grace of Body*.[2] Although the argument need not be conducted in the terms of sacramental theology, it does in my view provide one helpful avenue in, and so what I would like to do here is pursue that possibility under three general headings: the connection between enchantment and a more comprehensive notion of sacrament, objections to such a revised understanding, and finally some specific applications.

Enchantment and sacrament enlarged

In explaining why the topics mentioned above no longer occur in religious discussions in the way they once did, recourse might be had to a development that accelerated in the West from the sixteenth century onwards and which the sociologist Max Weber has called 'the disenchantment of the world'.[3] Theologians tend now only to know of his work in connection with *The Protestant Ethic and the Spirit of Capitalism* (1904–5), his influential and much contested account of the origins of capitalism. In that work the Reformation is seen as successfully extricating itself from a magical understanding of sacrament, Calvin in particular moving towards a purely instrumental view of its role. It is such instrumental rationality that Weber sees as characteristic of the modern world, and towards which he sees it as inexorably moving, as the advance of science eliminates mystery and puts explanation in its place. Things cease to be valued in their own right as mysteries and in their place the question is constantly of what role or further purpose they serve. With his own discipline of sociology part of this process, one might have thought that he would have viewed what was happening in entirely positive terms, but this is not so. He talks of human beings confined as it were 'in an iron cage', and, although he himself was without religious belief, he does seem to have felt that something was missing as a result, for he describes himself as 'religiously absolutely unmusical' and yet in this 'a cripple, a deformed human being'.[4]

Before examining other areas of human experience, it is worth thinking how this analysis might be applied to more conventional sacramental contexts, and in particular the eucharistic liturgy. Although in my view his critique is spoilt by an unremitting conservatism, the British sociologist Kieran Flanagan seems to me right in suggesting that much modern discussion of liturgy does reduce its role to one of mere function and instrumentality.[5] Instead of worship being pursued for its own sake, its purpose has come to be seen in primarily educative or missionary terms. So the question becomes what forms of worship are best for gearing up the congregation for evangelization in the world, or else making participants better informed about the contents of their faith rather than enabling them to bask in God's presence in and for its own sake. As an example of the trend, one might take the way in which metaphors with wide resonances from the old liturgy have been narrowed in scope in the mistaken desire for wider intelligibility. 'Lord, I am not worthy to receive you' has replaced the earlier 'Lord, I am not worthy that you should come under my roof'. Not only has the allusion to a gospel exchange been lost, but, more importantly, simple reception has replaced the more mysterious notion of indwelling.[6] Again, a common complaint against modern liturgy is its extreme wordiness, as doctrine is piled upon doctrine, with liturgy now seen as replacing the role once exercised by the sermon. Contemplation is thus replaced by one demand for commitment succeeding another. Fortunately, the human mind does not quite work like that. It can still put itself into contemplative mode even when language suggests otherwise and indeed find meanings unintended by the liturgist. Equally, religious buildings can still be experienced as having a meaning in their own right irrespective of how often it is insisted that they are only there to serve the liturgy. That latter matter is an issue to which I shall return towards the end of this essay, but I hope at least my main point is clear, the extent to which the Church has been its own worst enemy in endorsing purposive or instrumental rationality as the norm (Weber's *Zweckrationalität*) and so contributed to the further disenchantment of God's world (Weber's *Entzauberung*).

As I have already noted, Weber treats the Reformation as an important landmark in the process of disenchantment with the mystery and magic of sacraments replaced by either private mystery as in the case of Luther or pure instrumentality as with Calvin. Arguably, however, the process started much earlier for the Church, in particular at the turn of the first and second millennia as the Church responded to Berengar's challenges respecting the meaning of the Eucharist. In an important book Henri de Lubac has argued that, whereas in former times the three bodies (incarnational, eucharistic and ecclesiastical) had all been viewed as tightly bound together in single related unity but with the eucharistic body taken as the primary referent for the term *corpus mysticum*, now it was the Church that came to be described primarily in this way, with the eucharistic body treated as 'the real body', in theory a clarification but in practice, de Lubac suggests, a demotion.[7] For the net result was to move all the focus on to the nature of sacramental change in the symbol itself, and so to concentrate all the emphasis on questions of what brought about what instead of valuing the rite in the life of the believer in and for its own sake. This is not to say that the characteristically Aristotelian questions have no legitimacy, but it is to say that they encouraged an instrumentalism that could be seen as simply a staging post on the way to the Reformation. Some will find mystery an easier category in terms of which to discuss the Eucharist than others, but it is of course the nearest New Testament equivalent to the Latin word sacrament, and in church tradition the two terms did become virtually interchangeable. Neither Greek nor Latin Bibles use the terms directly of the two major Christian sacraments, but the way in which in Ephesians these are applied to marriage is often thought to require the narrower, specifically Christian meaning that came to be associated with the two words.[8] But by far the most common pattern of usage in the Scriptures is with reference to hinting symbols or types in which the old order is seen as an anticipation of the new: a hidden, partially comprehended sense that is only fully understood in retrospect.[9] It is that wider notion that, I think, helps explain the wide range of things and experiences which were labelled sacraments in the first millennium, before the term is finally narrowed down to the traditional seven under the decisive influence of Peter Lombard's *Sentences*. Augustine, for example, includes among his list of sacraments the Lord's Prayer, the Creed, the sign of the cross, ashes of penitence, oil of anointing, and even the Easter liturgy itself. All these signs offer a foretaste or anticipation of a larger reality. It is this notion of mediated participation that, I think, leads Augustine to concede that essentially the same phenomenon can occur outside Christianity no less than within. Thus we find him observing at one point that 'within no religious bond, whether true or false, can human beings be united, except they are bound together through some small symbol or visible sacrament'.[10] Many a modern writer has followed him, and so it is far from unusual to discover authorities on other major religions or even on long defunct ones finding the need to draw on the language of sacramentality.[11] Indeed, so marked is the parallel seen to be between the Christian sacraments and the sixteen rituals that mark the chief phases of a Hindu's life that the most commonly used textbooks introducing English children to Hinduism now translate the related term *samskara* simply as 'sacrament'.[12] Some of my fellow Christians may resent this apparent undermining of Christian distinctiveness, but I would contend that there is more gain than loss. It is not that everything labelled sacramental in this way must therefore now necessarily be endorsed by the Christian but rather that thereby the potential for a more positive estimate is indicated. Taking the doctrine of creation seriously generates an expectation that God will address his creation through its material reality, and that must surely mean all of humanity and not just those who are explicitly Christian. The use of *mysterion* in the New Testament commits the Christian to the existence of 'sacraments' already in the Old Testament, and so this might seem a natural extension of such a way of thinking. At all events, this wider conception for which I am appealing has been gaining pace throughout the twentieth century. Significant names in Anglicanism would include Charles Gore, Oliver Quick and William Temple, while since the Second Vatican Council it has become commonplace within Roman Catholicism to set discussion of the specific sacraments within the wider frame of Christ as the 'primordial sacrament' and the Church as the 'fundamental sacrament'. Initially such a frame might still appear narrowly Christian, but in fact in order to explicate why Christ should be described as the 'primordial sacrament' it soon becomes apparent that one must first give some independent way of identifying what the term means, and this is sometimes explicitly acknowledged. For example, one Catholic dictionary entry on sacraments opens with the declaration that 'sacramentality is not monopolized by Christianity; it extends to all human experience'.[13] So one way of approaching the type of experiences I mentioned at the beginning would be to widen the category of mystery and sacrament and use this as a means of exploring whether, as with the liturgy, a narrower focus on instrumental value has robbed modern Christianity of its ability to recognize in wider material experience a sense of divine presence conveyed in its own right.

Objections

In effect what I am pleading for is a new form of natural religion, taking seriously religious experiences within the Church that are not closely tied to any specific aspect of biblical revelation and parallel experience outside the Church of the many who lay claim to some form of encounter with God but yet seldom, if ever, darken a church's door. There are of course long-standing objections to this type of approach, particularly within Protestantism and Orthodoxy. The claim is that the world is fallen, and so cannot be read properly unless it is approached from the perspective of the Christian faith and not the other way round, and so the Christian sacraments should be seen as foundational for a correct perspective, not the culmination of some antecedent experiences. If Rahner and Tillich both allowed to some degree for the latter possibility, the twentieth century ended with two theologians in the ascendant, neither of whom would have been at all sympathetic to the type of approach I am advocating here: Barth and von Balthasar. Yet a puzzling paradox, if not contradiction, lies at the heart of both theologians' writings. On the one hand, we have God portrayed as marvellously generous in the way he has disclosed himself through the biblical revelation and in the Church; on the other, he speaks outside that revelation faintly and only then in a manner that acquires proper legitimacy and intelligibility when set in the context of the Christian faith. But if God is truly generous, would we not expect to find him at work everywhere and in such a way that all human beings could not only respond to him, however implicitly, but also develop insights from which even Christians could learn? Many theologians resist the logic of such a case because they believe that its implications will inevitably lead to a diminution of Christian conviction. But this is hardly inevitable. Indeed, in most cases the Bible has little to say on the areas of experience in question. Mention is made of some (such as architecture or music), but scarcely enough in itself to generate and require one particular perspective, while with others there is virtually nothing at all (1 Corinthians 9.24–27 could scarcely be used as a theoretical basis for observations on sport!). Nonetheless, the attempt is often made, but the result is usually shallow and unsatisfying, precisely because what is being canvassed is the imposition of presupposed general ideas rather than careful attention to the empirical data before any such interaction is attempted. Undoubtedly, however, the deeper worry is that the fallenness of the world is not being taken with sufficient seriousness and with it the absolute necessity of the prevenience of divine grace to save us. The legitimate criticism of Western medieval theology that it demoted grace by making it simply supervene on an independent nature has long since been well answered by a number of modern theologians, most notably perhaps by Karl Rahner himself.[14] Certainly the emphasis in the medieval period was wrong, but that should not lead to an undermining of the role of nature but rather to recognition of the way in which grace should be seen as always active, in nature no less than in revelation. Nature thus becomes, in Rahner's words, a mere *Restbegriff*, or 'remainder concept', an abstract term but never existing apart and by itself.[15]

But for some this is still not to go far enough. Grace may be in nature but it remains greatly inferior to what is given within the context of faith, and so nature must always be judged by the latter and never given some independent status. But will this do? Certainly, apparent sacramental activity outside Christianity can be culpable or idolatrous, but is it always so? Equally, the Christian sacraments undoubtedly do bring goodness and light, but is this always so? In short, do we not need to acknowledge a more complicated dynamic and see good and bad in both? Take a first experience outside Christianity. The fact that what is experienced gives only a partial understanding of God does not entail that it is therefore wrong. Were the experience in question claimed to be absolute, this would of course be so, but often that very partiality is fully acknowledged. Pagan myths, for example, are often made to tell apparently incompatible tales, precisely as a way of implicitly admitting their limitations. Again, even where the intention is evil as in Albert Speer's attempt to induce a religious awe in his proposed vast gathering hall for Nazi rallies in Berlin, it is not always the case that one needs explicit faith to see the wrongness of this.[16] A God-given conscience might detect that fault or evil just as well. Again, looking at matters from the other end, it just will not do for Christians always to assume the innate superiority of their own dispensation to whatever is given outside. Christian sacraments can also be instruments of corruption and evil. Later versions of the Catholic sacrament of confession, for instance, not only brought release and comfort to millions but perhaps to as many an increased sense of guilt and a manipulative power placed in the hands of their confessors. Again, in marked contrast to the doctrine of the incarnation, an increased sense of distance from God was actually the net result of infrequent Communion as practised in branches of the Christian Church as otherwise diverse as Orthodoxy and Calvinism, especially when combined, as it usually was, with assertion of a profound unworthiness to receive the sacrament. It is also the case that the Eucharist itself has sometimes functioned in an idolatrous or evil way. Think, for instance, of the misuse of excommunication in the medieval period or again of how more recently some liberation theologians have worried about open admission to Communion legitimating the actions of torturers and murderers in some of the former government tyrannies of South America.[17] So it cannot be the case that truth will only emerge by proceeding in one direction. The Church (and indeed the use of the Bible itself) stands in need of correction as well as what we might learn from the wider world. The obvious advantage, therefore, in starting from wider human experience is that in addressing the wider world one will not be first declaring it corrupt when it can only too easily see the corruptions within Christianity itself. Instead, the starting position becomes positive, what God is already doing in people's lives. The doctrine of Original Sin applies to us all. For too long it has been used to yield selective negative verdicts only on what happens outside the Church. Indeed, despite the prominent position given to the Fall in the opening chapters of Genesis, it is salutary to remind ourselves of how seldom that story is subsequently alluded to later in Scripture and by contrast how often a positive verdict is recorded on the natural world as a mediator of divine knowledge.[18]

Applications

Christianity is by no means the only religion in which communal meals, or blood and sacrifice, play a key role. In defending Christian doctrine in the patristic period, and again at the Renaissance, parallels were often drawn with pagan myths. Nowadays, it is often thought that the only proper defence is to stress difference, but the danger in absolute difference is irrelevance, the failure to touch where people are. However, I do not want to develop that point here nor the familiar appeal to experiences of God through nature but rather focus on some types that better illustrate how far the retreat from experiences that were once held to speak of the divine has in fact gone. Out of a very wide range of possible applications, I have chosen two: sport and architecture. If as late as the nineteenth century the issue of the religious significance of architecture was still the subject of serious debate, it was many centuries earlier that sport lost such a dimension. The contrast can quickly be seen by contrasting attitudes to the original Olympic Games (allegedly founded in 776 BC) and their modern revival (restored 1896). The former were essentially a religious celebration, as can be seen not only from the way in which each competitive event employed its own distinctive means of evoking the divine but also from the accompanying poetry of someone like Pindar.[19] The gods in his view do not merely bestow success, they also in the process grant grace of movement and bodily lustre that enables us to talk, I think, of something like sacramental participation in the life of the divine, with runner, charioteer or boxer opening a window in the human sphere on to the divine's own distinctive but different form of bodily reality. Even when due qualification is made for the fact that the gods' bodies are immortal, multi-locational and so forth, we are of course still at a huge remove from Christianity. Even so, that distance should not be exaggerated. Throughout Christian history the suffering servant's body 'without form or comeliness' has had to battle it out with an alternative conception, that Christ's body must necessarily have been physically beautiful, since he is by definition perfect humanity.[20] That is but one example out of many that might be used to illustrate a residual tendency within Christianity to continue to believe that God's presence is mediated through graced bodies. If such a view of sport was wholly abandoned, appeal to sculpture and ballet might still be used to demonstrate the issue continuing to bubble just beneath the surface. At times, perfection of form in sculpture or a transcendent leap in ballet can provide (at least for some) a real hint of God immanent in the world, just as on other occasions, despite all the hard work put in on the human side, there seems to be no parallel divine evocation (a phenomenon by no means uncommon also in the case of more conventional sacraments). That modern western instrumental attitudes to sport are not inevitable within developed religions is well illustrated by the markedly different history of some sports in the East, such as the martial arts, which probably originated in the sixth century AD in the Chinese Zen temple at Shaolin. That temple has now been revived, and in demonstrations offered across the world its monks have sought to stress the intimate connection that exists between Buddhism and such practices. Once again, there are considerable difficulties in translating from one religion to another, but, significantly, among those who make the attempt the language of 'sacrament' is not unknown, and indeed one author speaks of gaining access to 'the bottomless ground of Being', as one's body is 'breathed' through by the divine.[21] Just as in the ancient Olympic Games the aim was not just an instrumental one of achieving physical fitness or of demonstrating human superiority over others, so in these sports more than fitness, power or even integration of mind and body is at stake. The claim is that such practices offer access to a different level of reality, alignment with what Zen would call Buddha Nature.

The question of whether such a notion bears any relation to the Christian concept of God cannot possibly be pursued here. What can be observed is the current popularity of these sports in the West, with not merely the characteristic Western elements appropriated. The spiritual dimension is also commonly pursued. If the practise of more conventional western sports seems to offer few parallels and indeed with increasing commercialization to be travelling even further in the opposite direction, it is interesting to observe a number of film directors exploring contrary possibilities. In films such as Kevin Costner's 1989 *Field of Dreams* (about baseball), Norman Jewison's 1999 *The Hurricane* (about boxing) or Robert Redford's *Legend of Bagger Vance* (about golf) and quite a number of others, sport is clearly being treated as a means of experiencing the transcendent, and by that I understand more than merely human transcendence. Religious language and imagery, dramatic scenery and strange coincidences and appearances are all invoked to create a sense of a larger mysterious presence. Yet it is not as though any of the directors approach the issue from the perspective of committed Christian belief. Rather, they seem to be rebelling against a form of religion that has narrowly conceived religious experience, in order themselves to highlight one way in which an apparently purely human pull beyond one's present capacities can be met with a transcendent experience of a quite different order. The novelist John Updike is a rare example of a Christian who takes such questions seriously.[22] The irony is that many theologians, in their desire to protect the freedom of God not to be bound by his creation, deliberately exclude such half-way meetings from genuine experience of God, but failure to respond to searching humanity can scarcely be described as the act of a generous God. If worship is allowed to create or improve possibilities for encounter, why not also a nature that has become more focused as a result of human endeavour? Because architecture is an essentially human creation it is often supposed that it is incapable of mediating the divine or, if it does so, this is only because of the presence of a prayerful community or of artificially imposed signs that remind us of the biblical revelation (crosses and so forth).[23] The result is that it is often said that church architecture should never be judged in its own right but always only in so far as it serves the ends of the liturgy or of the liturgical community. Clergy and academics alike in plenty can be found, proffering just such a view. Such an instrumentalist understanding, however, denies what has certainly been a very common human experience in the past, and that is that architecture in itself and of its own right can mediate a sense of the presence of God. Read nineteenth-century discussions on the value of Gothic and one finds how passionate conviction on the matter could be, but it was not a conviction that first emerged then. Advocates of competing styles have often in the past put their claims in essentially religious terms, that one particular style captures best the essence of the divine nature. If in such arguments appeals to precedents allegedly set by the Temple are often surprisingly wide of the mark, modern scholarship does at least recognize extensive use of symbolism in that building, as also debates within Scripture about whether God's actual presence is thereby mediated or the building only a symbol for the divine 'name'.[24]

In trying to understand why a human artefact might mediate a sense of divine presence as strongly as something in the natural world or biblical revelation, perhaps a helpful parallel can be drawn with landscape painting. The kind of painter who seeks to give a religious dimension to some of his landscapes (artists such as Poussin, Constable, van Gogh or Cézanne) is at one level trying to induct us into a particular way of seeing the external world, but at another he is also attempting through the canvas itself to give us that experience. Similarly then with architecture; it is not that transcendence or immanence, order, exuberance or elegant simplicity are only conjured as existing elsewhere in what God has directly created, but that precisely because a relevant aspect of the divine character has been evoked, that aspect can now be experienced in and through the architecture itself. If this appears to bind the hand of God, as it were, it surely no more does so than in the principal Christian sacraments, where, there too, human beings engaged in doing something carries a promise of divine presence. To insist that nature could not carry such an implicit promise would seem to make an artificial distinction between one type of divine action and another. Biblical revelation and the natural world are alike creative acts with important ramifications. Because we live in such a means-orientated culture in which the types of experience noted above are seldom discussed, people are less used to conceptualizing what takes place. But that does not mean that such experiences have ceased to be common, nor that they are simply culturally determined. Just as incipient enjoyment of a classical symphony can be greatly enhanced if backed up with some induction into what the composer might be trying to achieve, so also could the religious dimension of architecture and the experience of God thereby be made possible, if more attention were given to such issues in their own right. There is not the space to pursue the matter here. All I can do is observe the way in which historic Western church art and architecture have often functioned as what the Germans call a *Gesamtkunstwerk*, that is a total experience with the architecture pulling in one direction and the art work in another, and thus very effectively complementing one another. To oversimplify, the transcendent soaring spires and pointed windows of Gothic architecture were balanced by the immanent realism of its sculptures, while in the earlier Romanesque style its artificially elongated, almost superhuman figures were nicely complemented by the earthly solidity and lateral thrust of its churches. God could thus be experienced as both transcendent and immanent without ever going beyond the experience of the building itself, into the celebration of the Mass and the preached word. That is not to say that other styles do not have their virtues or that more of God will not be discovered by going beyond the experience in question into what happens in the liturgy and preaching, but it is to insist that such experiences were once valued in their own right, and need to be so again. Precisely because builder or architect was trying to reflect key aspects of the nature of divine creativity, God could be experienced through their work no less forcibly than in the natural world itself or in the celebration of the biblical revelation.

In his novel *Oscar and Lucinda* the Australian novelist Peter Carey sends his clerical hero on a mad adventure to build a glass church in the Australian outback. Significantly, the test of the 'practical' is denounced as 'a word dull men use when they wish to hide the poverty of their imagination'.[25] Instead, the church is to be a 'celebration of God'. To put my thesis as provocatively and as simply as possible, it is this: it is a plea for the useless, for the material world of divine and human creation alike to be seen as capable of mediating experience of God, a sacramental reality to be valued in its own right irrespective of what further benefits it may bring. Without such an insistence worship itself will also eventually succumb to disenchantment, to mere instrumentality, whereas properly speaking, at its best, it too should be seen as useless, valued for the sacramental encounter it brings, not for whatever further alleged benefits may accrue.

Notes

1 In a recent article I have used John Drury and David Ford as examples of the failure to grant art its own integrity: 'God's glory revealed in art and music: learning from pagans' in M. D. Chapman (ed.), *Celebrating Creation* (London: Darton, Longman & Todd, 2004).

2 The first volume will be published by Oxford University Press in 2004.

3 See his essay 'Science as a vocation' in H. H. Gerth and C. Wright Mills (eds), *From Max Weber* (London: Routledge & Kegan Paul, 1948), pp. 129–56, esp. 155.

4 Quoted in L. A. Schaff, *Fleeing the Iron Cage* (Berkeley, CA: University of California Press, 1989), pp. 225–6.

5 *Sociology and Liturgy* (London: Macmillan, 1991); *The Enchantment of Sociology* (London: Macmillan, 1996).

6 The phrase was based originally on the centurion's response to Jesus: Matt. 8.6; Luke 7.6.

7 H. de Lubac, *Corpus mysticum: l'eucharistie et l'église au moyen age* (Paris: Aubier, 1949).

8 Eph. 5.31–2.

9 E.g., Mark 4.11–12; 1 Cor. 2.7–10; Col. 1.26–7; Rev. 1.20.

10 *Contra Faustum* 19.11 (my trans.).

11 For application to ancient religions generally, see E. O. James, *Sacrifice and Sacrament* (London: Thames & Hudson, 1962), esp. pp. 232–51.

12 E.g., V. P. Kanitkar, *Hinduism* (Cheltenham: Stanley Thornes & Hulton, 1989), pp. 18–29, esp. 20; V. Voiels, *Hinduism: A New Approach* (London: Hodder & Stoughton, 1998), pp. 92–8, esp. 92.

13 Bernard Cooke's entry in P. E. Fink (ed.), *The New Dictionary of Sacramental Worship* (Dublin: Gill & Macmillan, 1990), pp. 1116–23.

14 For a helpful analysis of the change, see E. Yarnold, *The Second Gift* (Slough: St Paul Publications, 1974).

15 K. Rahner, 'Concerning the relationship between nature and grace' in his *Theological Investigations* (London: Darton, Longman & Todd, 1961), I, pp. 297–317, esp. 302.

16 For Speer on the religious motivation, see his own *Inside the Third Reich* (New York: Macmillan, 1970), p. 153.

17 For some developments of the theme, see W. T. Cavanaugh, *Torture and Eucharist* (Oxford: Blackwell, 1998).

18 At times the treatment even appears mythological: cf. Ezek. 28.13–18. Passages like Rom. 3.23 and 5.19 surely need to be set in the context of the very positive estimate of the world given in the Wisdom literature.

19 For relevant details of the contests, see J. Swaddling, *The Ancient Olympic Games* (London: British Museum Press, 2nd edn, 1999); for some examples of Pindar using the language of grace, see *Olympians* X, 99–105; XI, 10; XIV, 1–13; *Nemeans* VI, 1–5.

20 Isa. 53.2. For a good contrast, see the poet-priest, Gerard Manley Hopkins' sermon for 23 November 1879, in W. H. Gardner (ed.), *Gerard Manley Hopkins: A Selection of his Poetry and Prose* (Harmondsworth: Penguin, 1953), pp. 137–9.

21 J. Stevens, *The Secrets of Aikido* (Boston: Shambhala, 1997), pp. 29, 121; E. Herringel, *Zen in the Art of Archery* (London: Penguin, 1985), esp. pp. 14, 17, 36.

22 J. Updike, *Golf Dreams* (London: Penguin, 1996), e.g., pp. 125, 147, 151.

23 For a good statement of such a perspective, see S. White, 'The Theology of Sacred Space' in D. Brown and A. Loades (eds), *The Sense of the Sacramental* (London: SPCK, 1995), pp. 31–43.

24 For Temple symbolism, see M. Barker, *The Gate of Heaven* (London: SPCK, 1991); *The Great High Priest* (London: T&T Clark, 2003); for the contrast between passages such as Exod. 29.45; Ps. 68.16; Ezek. 43.5 and many others with the anti-sacramental approach of the Deuteronomist: G. von Rad, 'Deuteronomy's "Name" Theology and the Priestly Document's "Kabod" Theology' in *Studies in Deuteronomy* (Naperville, Ill.: Allenson, 1953), pp. 37–46.

25 P. Carey, *Oscar and Lucinda* (London: Faber & Faber, 1988), pp. 388, 390–91.

3

Contemporary culture and the reinvention of sacramental spirituality

John Drane

Thirty years ago, it was more or less taken for granted that by the end of the twentieth century the Christian Church – along with organized religion in all its forms – would be relegated to the lunatic fringes of society, if not extinct altogether. The secularization thesis prevailed, and it seemed as if nothing could stop the inexorable march of civilized people towards a non-religious future. Though that opinion still has its exponents,[1] they are a diminishing minority, for one of the most remarkable and unexpected features of life in the twenty-first century is what has been referred to as 'the desecularization of the world'.[2] In the Christian context, the Church is not only surviving, but thriving and growing, largely under the influence of the Pentecostal-Charismatic movement, which did not even exist until a hundred years ago.[3] Paradoxically, however, though more than three-quarters of the English population declared themselves to be 'Christian' in the 2001 census, that allegiance (if that is the right way of describing it) does not translate into any significant level of religious observance, whether Christian or any other.[4] The same phenomenon is present throughout the Western world, and it has become a cliché to observe that while people

37

may be less 'religious' they are apparently more 'spiritual'. My aim here is to reflect on this trend in relation to the ongoing life and mission of the Church. Crisis is not too strong a word to describe the predicament of the Church in the West. Desperate days call for desperate measures and, as Michael Riddell counsels, 'This is a time which calls for courage and experimentation'.[5] In following that advice, I quite deliberately present some ideas that may be less than fully formed, in the effort to identify new directions that may be worth further exploration and reflection.

Doing theology

In the title of his book *Who we are is how we pray*,[6] Charles Keating reminded his readers of an inescapable reality of all reflective enquiry, namely that the interpreter and his or her subject can never quite be separated from one another. The notion of the autonomous rational individual pursuing knowledge in a disinterested way is not only unworkable, but actually diminishes the value of human experience and in the process produces an impoverished epistemology which ignores some of the most important questions of all. It is therefore entirely appropriate – indeed necessary – to begin with the prior experience that I bring to this topic. As a practical theologian, I regard theology not as an intrinsically cerebral affair, but first and foremost as something to be 'done'. There is a substantial ongoing debate about the nature of this discipline and though there is no absolute consensus, most would locate it within a praxis-reflection method with roots in the insights of liberation theology, feminist theology and other approaches which prioritize the experience of people as the launching pad from which new questions might be addressed to the Christian tradition in order to articulate appropriately theological perspectives on today's world.[7]

My own hermeneutical frame of reference has been shaped by several personal factors. For twenty-five years I taught in the Religious Studies department of a secular university, where students typically expressed a profound distrust of institutional Christianity, while being intensely curious about what they often described as the 'real' meaning of the Gospel. The latter – in so far as it could be identified – might play a significant part in their own search for spiritual meaning, while the former was invariably dismissed out of hand. That experience convinced me that we cannot meaningfully talk about Christian sacramentality without also valuing the faith journeys of those who belong to no particular tradition, and whom Christians and social scientists alike might regard as 'secular'. Over the same period, my Christian ministry became increasingly ecumenical, in every sense of that word – reminding me that any narrowly sectarian view of faith (including my own) was bound to be limiting, if not distorting. Then in my personal life I had to cope with the death of my daughter, which forced me to ask questions in a completely new way. Traditional arguments about theodicy became irrelevant, as I found my worldview turned upside down by the way in which my wife found healing in that situation. Having been a medical researcher, she became a clown – more than that, a clown minister – and as I witnessed the power of this form of Christian ministry not only to inspire but also to transform her own life and that of others,[8] I began to question the entire rational undergirding of what I thought I was doing, ending up less confident in the power of words, and more conscious of the importance of image, relationships and emotions as intrinsic aspects of what it means to be human and whole.[9] Influenced by all these factors, I have chosen to take a broad view of the topic under consideration here, combining threads from disparate parts of contemporary culture, each of which has its own specialized scholarly discourse. In the process of doing so, I inevitably make generalizations that might require more careful qualification, or may even be unsustainable when placed alongside actual situations or viewpoints. At the same time, however, my prior experience suggests that this is a creative way of gaining some sense of perspective on the emerging sacramentality of popular culture. What is offered, therefore, is a compass, not a detailed road map – suggesting a general sense of the territory rather than focusing on specifics. Tom Beaudoin succinctly expresses the theological assumption behind this approach with his observation that

> people who profess to know little or nothing about the religious may indeed form, inform, or transform religious meaning for people of faith . . . The kingdom of God is constantly revealed and enacted through the least likely person or circumstances. If the first are to be last and the last first, then popular culture itself, as a quintessential instance of what counts as 'last' in importance for many cultural high priests, may be granted its moment of significance.[10]

Andrew Greely is even more explicit:

> If one believes that people are sacraments of God, that God discloses himself/herself to us through objects, events, and persons of life, then one must concede the possibility that in the sacramentality of ordinary folk, their hopes, their fears, their loves, their aspirations represent a legitimate experience of God, legitimate symbols of God, and legitimate stories of God.[11]

More recently, Craig Detweiler and Barry Taylor have tantalizingly suggested that 'sacramental churches are poised for a comeback'[12] – a claim that might sound like good news for at least some Christian traditions, until we reflect on their further recommendation:

> It is time to take the consecrated bread out of the tabernacle and place it in the hands of ordinary people, offering them a new portrait of holiness. Popular culture continues to redefine the relationship between the sacred and the secular, the holy and the profane. People of faith should do the same.[13]

Popular culture

Before returning to these questions, we must take time to reflect on contemporary popular culture, which is both the product of and the catalyst for an enormous upheaval of norms and values throughout the Western world (and thence, through the influence of globalization, to everywhere else). The academy tends to regard this move from 'modernity' to 'postmodernity' (with or without the hyphen) as a philosophically determined shift, but that understanding is the product of a 'high' culture that assumes things will change as intellectuals promote new ideas, which then percolate downwards and ultimately affect the lives of ordinary people. There are obviously connections between postmodern philosophy and the experiences of everyday life, but one does not necessarily lead to the other. Many people live without having – or feeling any need to have – a framework going beyond their own experience and what 'feels right'. For centuries, a common language was provided by Graeco-Roman philosophical categories which, because of their nature, required intellectuals to interpret the world authoritatively on behalf of others. That shared language has gone, replaced by a fluid world-view rooted not in high culture but in the popular media culture which is now the everyday language of the street and the home – and which is not determined by 'those who know best' but is open to change and constant reappraisal by every individual to suit their own circumstances and life experience. Zygmunt Bauman captures this well with his image of 'liquid modernity', contrasting the 'solid modernity' of previous centuries as 'an era of mutual engagement' with what he calls 'fluid modernity' as 'the epoch of disengagement'.[14] When the two are compared at a pragmatic level, it is clear that 'postmodernity' (or whatever other label is given to today's emerging culture) is about much more than a loss of shared understanding in the face of new questions: it is a completely different way of understanding what the world is about – and in spiritual terms, represents a new model of sensory-religious imagination in which 'the ways of being religious are moving out of the protected sphere of relig-ious institution and tradition, and into the open ground of the symbolic marketplace'.[15] In a presentation to the Catholic Theological Society of America in 1998, Lynn Schofield Clark argued passionately that Christians cannot afford to ignore the reality of this popular culture as the 'source' and 'primary lan-guage for meaning' in today's world.[16]

41

Several characteristics of popular postmodernity are of particular significance in relation to the emergence of new forms of sacramentality. Foremost among these is an increasing sense of self-reliance, which is the natural outcome of the experience of living in a culture which is increasingly characterized by untrustworthy persons and institutions. For forty-four days during September and October 2003 illusionist David Blaine was suspended in a glass box by the River Thames in London, with only water to sustain him. Though some derided his endeavour, even using criminal means to try and bring it to a premature end, many more found themselves strangely attracted by this spectacle and what it represented. For here was a man pushing himself to the limit, to test how far he could trust himself in a world where everything else was unreliable. The essentially spiritual nature of his attempt becomes clearer when understood in the context of his previous stunts. One of these involved being frozen in a block of ice for almost three days, while another one required him to stand for two days on top of a pillar only 22 inches in diameter and 109 feet from the ground, without food, water, sleep or physical support. All these things can find precedents, if not exact parallels, in the behaviour of mystics within the historic Christian tradition. Extreme sports are increasingly popular for similar reasons: they offer opportunities for individuals to assess their own trustworthiness in a world of mutual suspicion.[17] The rise of the so-called 'New Age' is another manifestation of the same concerns. The view that this kind of self-defined sacramentality is pathologically destructive and ultimately meaningless is shared by people as diverse as religion scholar Paul Heelas, neo-fundamentalist Carl Trueman, and journalist Roland Howard,[18] while some Christians regard it as dangerously occult, and its practitioners as demon possessed.[19] I regard all these opinions as theologically indefensible and missiologically suicidal.[20] Reliance on oneself is the inevitable outcome of a worldview that in the last two or three centuries has systematically removed the possibility of transcendence from our lives, leaving us with nothing but ourselves as the touchstone of authenticity. Once that worldview itself no longer makes sense, and when we then look within we find nothing but emptiness and meaninglessness, it is only natural to explore anything that looks as if it might offer help with our existential questions. This is not a self-centred choice, representing the ultimate hubris of human beings who believe themselves to be in the place of God, but is the ultimate despair of a race that is bereft of meaning and identity – less sinning and more sinned against by its inherited culture which has promoted what David Hay evocatively calls 'the social destruction of spirituality'.[21]

This in turn has produced a growing impatience with all rational ways of being, since they appear not to have delivered what they promised. People are not happier and more fulfilled than previous generations: indeed they feel increasingly trapped in 'McDonaldized' systems.[22] Nor is the world perceived as self-evidently a better place through the development of science and technology. Moreover, the inherited Western paradigm is widely regarded as fractured and disconnected, highlighting the need for holistic ways of being that can deal with personal fragmentation as well as larger cosmic, cultural and even scientific understandings.[23]

Michel de Certeau has emphasized the importance of practices of everyday life in understanding the spiritual search of today's people.[24] Several practices, or attitudes, are worth noting before we move on to consider how this affects the Christian tradition. Because we no longer trust prescriptive ways of being, we find it difficult to trust religious institutions and the rationalized sacramentality which they offer.[25] Alongside this is a profound questioning of the nature of truth as propositions, for that in itself can too easily become a fragmenting influence. 'Faith' is more likely to be understood as a verb rather than a noun, and non-rational experiences (tactile, visual, emotional) are likely to be prioritized over the exclusively rational. There is a concern for relational wholeness, searching for personal healing and community in the midst of life's brokenness, but developing new forms of both rather than accepting what already exists, which tends to be seen as false and meaningless, and quite possibly controlling and exploitational.

If the self is the only core essence left to us, it is only natural for people to desire a new connection with primal instincts and intuitions, on the assumption that 'if there is something out there, it will be accessed in the first place by my experiences in here'. What is personal becomes a gateway to the transcendent, and therefore sacramental in a very precise sense.[26] This is often accompanied by a questioning of dualism as a useful category of understanding, though monism is not as widespread in popular spirituality as some commentators assume.[27] All this might sound like a re-emergence of what Aldous Huxley called 'the perennial philosophy'[28] but whereas for him it was essentially a speculative, rationally focused project, for today's spiritual searchers it is more experientially based, an effort to identify spiritual tools to overcome one's hurts and realize one's hopes, to empower people to live effectively through a spiritual awakening – all of which might be accomplished by sampling from a range of spiritual tools or disciplines so as to create sacramental experiences.

Everyday Sacramentality

To illustrate the nature of the challenge faced by the Christian Churches, we must consider some specific ways in which people are searching for sacramental meaning without the constraints of rationalized structures. There are many examples to choose from, such as aromatherapy (a form of chrism?), psychotherapy (confession?), rebirthing (baptism?), or any number of other 'alternative' therapies, while a leading practical theologian has recently characterized 'spiritual caregiving' as a 'secular sacrament'.[29] But one of the most accessible expressions of popular sacramentality is in club culture and pop music. Those who never frequent clubs tend to regard them as a young person's habitat, though in reality they represent a widespread 'alternative' culture unrestricted by either generation or social class. When Sheryl Garratt claimed that 'Clubs are the churches of the new millennium' she was not exaggerating.[30] Many clubs in the UK are housed in former church buildings, and often use that fact to create a sacramental ethos. In Scotland alone, I have personal knowledge of clubs with names like '*The Church*', '*Joy*', '*God's Kitchen*', '*Angel*', '*Spirit*', '*Paradise*', '*Ministry of Sin*', '*The Sunday Service*', and '*Ascension*'. Though few clubbers would have any idea what most of that means, the use of symbolic language drawn from an otherwise meaningless Christian past serves to impart a sense of 'mystery' if not 'sacredness' to the experience. Conversely, the clubbing experience itself offers most of the ingredients of church at its best: regular attendance at events with no other purpose beyond themselves, rituals of preparation (choosing appropriate clothes, arranging transportation, putting money aside), and a sense of belonging, participation, acceptance and openness to others that is quite different from what is on offer in any other social context. Clubbers can even have the equivalent of the mystical experience that the Church offers through the Eucharist, encountered in this case either through an 'oceanic experience' (the atmosphere)[31] or through the use of drugs (most notably Ecstasy which, like the wafer of the Eucharist – and unlike most other recreational drugs – is ingested through the mouth and comes with a mystical symbol embossed in it).

It would be easy to dismiss these parallels between church and club culture as the exaggerations of an over-active imagination were it not for the fact that much dance music specifically articulates such concepts. One of the most outstanding examples of this is the album *Sunday 8pm* by Faithless.[32] As well as songs alluding to biblical stories, with titles like '*The Garden*', '*Hour of Need*', '*Take the long way Home*', or '*Hem of his Garment*', '*God is a DJ*' explicitly identifies club with church, describing the experience as one of healing, community-building, and transcendence. Though we celebrate the collapse of those traditional institutions which offered us safety and security, we are apparently terrified of the prospects for individual survival – let alone flourishing – in a world that has as a result become depersonalized and in which, instead of being at the mercy of accountable systems, our lives are now determined by the needs of multinational corporations and market forces. This societal meltdown is creating 'an unholy trinity of uncertainty, insecurity and unsafety'[33] but because of our distrust of rationalized structures, we deal with these needs on an occasional basis, and the club offers an appropriately impersonal vehicle for transcending personal fragmentation at that moment in time. By offering a glimpse of the meaning and spiritual purpose that we believe ourselves increasingly unlikely to achieve in this lifetime, the sacramentality of the club also offers an eschatological dimension. Christians are not absent from this scene. An accessible example of creative Christian engagement is the Clubbers Temple, a website operated by a UK group which sends teams of Christians to work among the clubbers at the Spanish resort of Ibiza, widely regarded as the club capital of Europe.[34] The website is designed as a virtual community for those who are engaged in the spiritual search but would be unlikely to connect with a local church. Entering the Temple creates the experience of going through the doors of a real club with music, dance, and so on. It describes itself as a place of search, feeling, and experience: 'Clubbers Temple is for those who know there's more to life . . . for those who believe the truth is out there and the invisible is more real than the visible.' It would be hard to improve on that as a description of what we mean by 'sacramentality'! The site then offers an invitation to enter three separate rooms, 'Thirst', 'Beach', and 'Words'. 'Thirst' is 'a place for you to re-connect with the divine source of all life', and on entering it one encounters a room with a picture of a desert on the wall, which turns out to be a hyperlink to a visualization that then leads the visitor through the desert, to discover an oasis with warm, dirty water before encountering 'the guardian of the pool' who offers fresh sparkling water, and invites the curious to drink from his bottle, which turns out to be another hyperlink that takes the bottle back to the original room and places it on the table. A statement links this to biblical themes ('the spiritual water that Jesus offers will refresh and replenish your body, soul, mind and spirit'), followed by an invitation: 'If you choose to follow Jesus, your spiritual thirst will be quenched, you can experience Jesus right here, right now, if you desire.' By choosing the option 'more' (rather than 'exit'), one can empty the bottle while seeing these words: 'Jesus I am thirsty, I need to drink your living water. Please come and refresh my life now.' The next question is: 'What happened? What did you feel?' Whatever one might think of all this, it is unquestionably offering a sacramental experience. Like the sanctuary of a church (and a club), the website itself is consciously designed to be a spiritual space. Moreover, there is an intentionality about creating a sacramental experience: one of the other rooms invites visitors to 'let the music take you deeper into God's presence'. It is also aiming to build community online, as can be seen by the chat rooms and bulletin boards on the site. To complete the picture, it seems to 'work'. On the day I visited the site, one of the comments on the bulletin board read: 'I logged on, and wow, I can feel God through this'.[35]

It hardly needs to be said that not everyone is self-consciously interested in searching for spiritual meaning in life.[36] But there is undoubtedly a significant – and expanding – group of such people within Western populations, who offer a particular opportunity – and challenge – to the Christian Church, for several reasons. For one thing, they are well represented, maybe over-represented, by personalities who feature in the media, and that in itself means they are taken seriously and their views are widely disseminated. They apparently include establishment figures such as Cherie Blair, wife of the British Prime Minister, who has been reported connecting with spirit guides and alter-native healers, and undergoing a rebirthing ritual (in the latter case accompanied by her husband) – and before her, Princess Diana was devoted to much the same things. They are joined by various Hollywood movie stars, whose stories of spiritual search are well enough documented, not to mention postmodern nov-elists such as Douglas Coupland.[37] These spiritual searchers also tend to be people who, in socio-economic terms, would have been most actively involved in the life of the Church in past gen-erations. Indeed, many have themselves been members of the Church at one time or another, but find it no longer meets their spiritual needs.[38] No longer lay leaders in local congregations, they put their energies into single-issue pressure groups, as well as engaging in more overtly 'spiritual' therapies and self-defined sacramental activities.[39] Surprisingly, perhaps, the more their claims are subjected to scientific scrutiny, the more support they attract. Scientists promoting an overtly sacramental view of life include mystic Fritjof Capra who claims that physics is merely a branch of Eastern monism,[40] along with the less sensational – though probably more influential – medic Andrew Newberg, who believes that we are all genetically programmed to be 'spiritual'.[41] Then there is David Hay, whose mentor Alister Hardy claimed that spirituality is in some way biologically conditioned, if not determined, and whose own recent research has itself highlighted the spirituality of those who operate outside traditional faith communities.[42] This kind of research poses a particular challenge for the Church in terms of knowing how to recognize and affirm those sacramental meeting points between the material and the transcendent. For 'sacramentality' is, in this sense, a universal human quality, seen in sports, shopping and many other apparently 'secular' activities, some of which parallel the sense of awe and wonder of the holy days of the liturgical calendar.[43] In terms of the Church's mission, it emphasizes the importance of asking, not 'how can we make people spiritual?' – (Because they already are) – but rather, 'how can we connect with their innate spirituality and point them towards Christ?'

Opportunities for the Church

It would take an entire book to unpack all the challenges this presents to the churches. Here I simply list some of the key areas that Christian theology must address. First and foremost must be the rediscovery of some kind of creation-centred spirituality. Beaudoin observes that Gen X-ers (the particular subject of his study) 'live a theology revolving around the incarnation . . . and express religiosity with *sacramentals* which can evoke the religious depth of the most common objects or experiences'.[44] A similar argument for a re-orientation of theological priorities in favour of the doctrines of creation and Incarnation has, of course, been most forcefully advanced by Matthew Fox,[45] though he misses what Beaudoin emphasizes, namely that 'sacramentals' are a way of dealing with pain. By marginalizing, if not eliminating, the fall/redemption trajectory, Fox tends to downplay the reality of suffering and the cosmic nature of sin.[46] In a post-9/11 world, that is no longer possible: the two need to go hand-in-hand. Alongside this, and running parallel with it, is a need for a missiological reorientation in the Church's attitude to the innate sacramentality of those who are not Christians. There is a biblical precedent for this in the account of St Paul's visit to Athens (Acts 17.16–34), where the apostle regarded such activities in a positive light as 'altars to the unknown god' whose story he then proceeded to share. But there is also a historical sense of déjà vu here, for in the early centuries a multiplicity of experiences could be regarded as sacramental. Augustine, for example, described the ashes of Ash Wednesday as a 'sacrament', though by the thirteenth century that was no longer possible and in the post-Reformation period the options were even more severely limited. This observation highlights what is perhaps one of the most fundamental questions of all for Christian theology in the context of popular culture, namely, what is the appropriate starting point for doing theology? To put it simply, which comes first: Christian discipleship (following Jesus), or cognitive propositions about God? Though it might be over-optimistic to imagine that in the earliest centuries spiritual experience was the only influence shaping the sacramental life of Christians, it is certainly the case that by the sixteenth century, in Protestantism most obviously but also to a lesser extent in the Roman Catholic tradition following the Council of Trent (1545–1563), it was increasingly supposed that believing should shape behaviour, and that abstract theology would determine the nature of experience rather than the other way round. Though the Reformers generally held to some transcendent understanding of the sacraments, when all this was combined with the philosophical rationalism of the Enlightenment, it was virtually inevitable that the notion that material objects and actions might have spiritual connections should be dismissed as nonsensical. Kant was not alone in regarding such a notion as 'religious illusion which can do naught but work counter to the spirit of religion'.[47] Whether intentionally or not, most Protestants have allowed this approach to dominate their understanding of the sacraments and have preferred to regard them as moralistic reminders of the past work of Christ rather than offering any kind of direct encounter with him today. The early Methodists, with their understanding of baptism in terms of regeneration, and Eucharist as a converting ordinance, were the exceptions, though that emphasis disappeared over time. In theory, the Pentecostal tradition should be in a position to engage with this, though in the understandable effort to make itself acceptable to historic mainstream Christianity it has adopted the same rationalistic outlook, and in the process has tended to minimize the importance of the symbolic and ritualistic in favour of the cognitive and propositional.

There is also an opportunity for the Church to reconnect sacrament and story in order to establish meaningful connections with the kind of sacramentality represented by the self-determined spiritual pathways mentioned above. In his critique of Protestantism, Paul Tillich issued what might now be regarded as a prophetic call for 'a rediscovery of the sacramental space' as the key to the very future of the Church, insisting that this should involve the recognition that 'natural objects can become bearers of transcendent power and meaning . . . by being brought into the context of the history of salvation'.[48] For the one thing that is missing from self-defined sacramentality is an awareness of the bigger story which gives meaning to it all. Though the philosophers insist that 'incredulity toward meta-narratives'[49] is a characteristic of post-modernity, the actual evidence calls for a more nuanced understanding, and suggests that, while we have rejected the traditional meta-narrative of Western 'high' culture, popular culture is not rejecting the possibility that there might be such a story, but is rather searching for a new one that more closely approximates to the realities of everyday life.[50] In this context, Christians can usefully echo the question posed by Philip the evangelist (Acts 8.30), and ask of those who are reinventing a sacramental worldview, 'Do you understand what you are doing?' – followed up by a creative telling of the Gospel story, within the media framework of popular culture. Finally, any meaningful missiological engagement with so-called secular sacramentality must take full account of the way that so many people are traumatized by social and relational instability. Though the causes are different, we experience at least as much personal pain as all previous generations – some would say more. Though we lack a sense of meaning, we also declare a significant interest in pursuing meaning.[51] Douglas Coupland speaks eloquently for many when he identifies our need 'to tell stories and to make our own lives worthwhile tales in the process'.[52] Christian theology began with the telling of stories, so this invitation should be neither novel nor threatening. It invites us not to explain, but to acknowledge, and perhaps even celebrate, the insecurities of the human condition, something which a reimagined Christian sacramentality ought to be able to accomplish very easily.

Notes

1 Notably Steve Bruce, *God is Dead: Secularization in the West* (Oxford: Blackwell, 2002).

2 Peter Berger (ed.), *The Desecularization of the World* (Grand Rapids: Eerdmans, 1999).

3 Cf. Allan H. Anderson and Walter J. Hollenweger, *Pentecostals after a Century: Global Perspectives on a Movement in Transition* (Sheffield: Sheffield Academic Press, 1999); David Martin, *Pentecostalism: the World their Parish* (Oxford: Blackwell, 2001); Murray Dempster, Byron D. Klaus, Douglas Petersen (eds), *The Globalization of Pentecostalism: a Religion Made to Travel* (Oxford: Regnum, 1999).

4 Cf. Peter Brierley, *UK Christian Handbook: Religious Trends 4* (London: Christian Research, 2003).

5 Michael Riddell, *Threshold of the Future* (London: SPCK, 1998), p. 2.

6 Charles Keating, *Who we are is how we pray* (Mystic CT: Twenty-Third Publications, 1987).

7 On the nature of practical theology, see Paul Ballard and John Pritchard, *Practical Theology in Action: Christian Thinking in the*

Service of Church and Society (London: SPCK, 1996); James Woodward and Stephen Pattison (eds), *The Blackwell Reader in Pastoral and Practical Theology* (Oxford: Blackwell, 1999). This is not the place to justify my own approach, except to note that it is similar to that of Don Browning, *A Fundamental Practical Theology: Descriptive and Strategic Proposals* (Minneapolis: Fortress Press, 1991).

8 Cf. O. M. Fleming Drane, *Clowns, Storytellers, Disciples* (Oxford: BRF, 2002).

9 A wider cultural trend eloquently described by Mitchell Stephens, *The Rise of the Image, the Fall of the Word* (New York: Oxford University Press, 1998).

10 Tom Beaudoin, *Virtual Faith: The Irreverent Spiritual Quest of Generation X* (San Francisco: Jossey-Bass, 1998), pp. 34, 32.

11 Andrew M. Greeley, *God in Popular Culture* (Chicago: Thomas More Press, 1988), p. 15.

12 Craig Detweiler and Barry Taylor, *A Matrix of Meanings: Finding God in Pop Culture* (Grand Rapids: Baker, 2003), p. 301.

13 Ibid., p. 291.

14 Zygmunt Bauman, *Liquid Modernity* (Cambridge: Polity Press, 2000), p. 120.

15 Stewart M. Hoover, 'Religion, Media and the Cultural Center of Gravity', an address to the Trustees of the Foundation for United Methodist Communications, 7 May 1998. See the website of the International Study Commission on Media, Religion, and Culture: http://www.colorado.edu/Journalism/MEDIALYF/analysis/umcom.html

16 Lynn Schofield Clark, 'Building Bridges between Theology and Media Studies', on the International Study Commission on Media, Culture and Religion website: http://www.jmcommunications.com/english/clark2.htm

17 See Shirl J. Hoffman, *Sport and Religion* (Champaign IL: Human Kinetics Books, 1992), pp. 63–75.

18 Paul Heelas, *The New Age Movement* (Oxford: Blackwell, 1996); Roland Howard, *Shopping for God* (London: HarperCollins, 2001); Carl Trueman, 'Boring ourselves to Life', in *Themelios* 28/3 (2003), pp. 1–4.

CULTURE AND SACRAMENTAL SPIRITUALITY

19 Constance Cumbey, *The Hidden Dangers of the Rainbow* (Lafayette LA: Huntington House, 1983); Douglas Groothuis, *Confronting the New Age* (Downers Grove, IL: InterVarsity Press, 1988); Alan Morrison, *The Serpent and the Cross* (Birmingham: K & M Books, 1994).

20 I am not alone in this: cf. Richard Harries, *God outside the Box* (London: SPCK, 2002).

21 David Hay with Rebecca Nye, *The Spirit of the Child* (London: Fount, 1998), pp. 21–39.

22 Cf. George Ritzer, *McDonaldization: The Reader* (Thousand Oaks CA: Pine Forge Press, 2002).

23 An analysis first presented by Jan Christiaan Smuts, *Holism and Evolution* (New York: Macmillan, 1926), and more recently popularized especially through the writings of a new breed of knowledge entrepreneurs who recycle discrete specialist perspectives into whole-systems views that go beyond the bare facts to explore what the facts might actually mean to those wishing to see the bigger pictures. Cf. for example, Gregory and Mary Catherine Bateson, *Angels Fear: Towards an Epistemology of the Sacred* (New York: Bantam, 1988); Fritjof Capra, *The Web of Life: A New Synthesis of Mind and Matter* (San Francisco: HarperCollins, 1996); Arthur Koestler, *The Sleepwalkers: A History of Man's Changing Vision of the Universe* (London: Hutchinson, 1959); Rupert Sheldrake, *A New Science of Life: The Hypothesis of Formative Causation* (London: Flamingo, 1995, 2nd edn); Danah Zohar, *Rewiring the Corporate Brain: Using the New Science to rethink how we structure and lead Organizations* (San Francisco: Berrett-Koehler Publishers, 1997); Shoshana Zuboff, *In the Age of the Smart Machine: The Future of Work and Power* (Oxford: Heinemann, 1988).

24 Michel de Certeau, *The Practice of Everyday Life* (Berkeley: University of California Press, 1984).

25 On the rationalized spirituality of the Church, see John Drane, *The McDonaldization of the Church* (London: Darton, Longman & Todd, 2000).

26 In applying the term 'sacramental', I am adopting the definition proposed by James F. White, *The Sacraments in Protestant Practice and Faith* (Nashville: Abingdon Press, 1999), p. 13, as the idea that 'the

outward can convey the inward and spiritual' in such a way that physical actions become a meeting place with the transcendent.

27 Cf. Paul Greer, 'The Aquarian Confusion: Conflicting Theologies of the New Age', in *Journal of Contemporary Religion* 10/2 (1995), pp. 151–66.

28 A Huxley, *The Perennial Philosophy* (New York: Harper, 1944).

29 Ray S. Anderson, *Spiritual Caregiving as Secular Sacrament* (London: Jessica Kingsley, 2003).

30 Sheryl Garratt, *Adventures in Wonderland: a Decade of Club Culture* (London: Headline, 1998), p. 305.

31 The expression of Ben Malbon, *Clubbing: Dancing, Ecstasy and Vitality* (London: Routledge, 1999), p. 106. The Theologian Tex Sample similarly describes the experience of dance as 'a kind of transcendence . . . One is taken out of the ordinary, routine world . . . It is another time and place. It has a spiritual and meditative quality about it.' Cf. *The Spectacle of Worship in a Wired World* (Nashville: Abingdon, 1998), p. 71.

32 Faithless, *Sunday 8pm* (London: Cheeky Records, 1998).

33 Bauman, *Liquid Modernity*, p. 181.

34 http://www.clubberstemple.com

35 Another example of a similar Christian effort to connect with club culture and popular spirituality can be seen in 24/7 boiler house prayer rooms. See http://www.boiler-rooms.com

36 In *McDonaldization of the Church*, pp. 55–84, I identified seven people groups, half of which would by definition not match this profile.

37 See, e.g., Douglas Coupland, *Generation X* (New York: St Martin's Press, 1991); *Life after God* (New York: Simon & Schuster 1994); *Polaroids from the Dead* (London: Flamingo, 1996); and several more.

38 Alan Jamieson, *A Churchless Faith* (London: SPCK, 2002).

39 Cf. Paul Vallely, 'Evangelism in a post-religious society', in *Setting the Agenda: The Report of the 1999 Church of England Conference on Evangelism* (London: Church House Publishing, 1999), pp. 30–43.

40 Fritjof Capra, *The Tao of Physics: An Exploration of the Parallels between Modern Physics and Eastern Mysticism* (London: Wildwood House, 1975).

41 Andrew Newberg, *Why God Won't Go Away: Brain Science and the Biology of Belief* (New York: Ballantine Books, 2002); cf. Eugene G. D'Aquili and Andrew B. Newberg, *The Mystical Mind: Probing the Biology of Religious Experience* (Minneapolis: Augsburg, 1999).

42 David Hay and Kate Hunt, *Understanding the Spirituality of People who don't go to Church* (Nottingham: University of Nottingham School of Education, 2000).

43 See Ira G Zepp, *The New Religious Image of Urban America: The Shopping Mall as Ceremonial Center* (Niwot CO: University Press of Colorado, 1997, 2nd ed.); Shirl J. Hoffman, *Sport and Religion* (Champaign IL: Human Kinetics Books, 1992).

44 Beaudoin, *Virtual Faith*, p. 74.

45 Matthew Fox, *Original Blessing* (Santa Fé: Bear & Co, 1983).

46 For a critique of Fox, see John Drane, 'Fox, Matthew' in Trevor Hart (ed.), *The Dictionary of Historical Theology* (Carlisle: Paternoster Press, 2000), pp. 218–20.

47 That is, 'religion', as he defined it: cf. his *Religion within the Limits of Reason Alone* (English translation, New York: Harper & Row, 1960), p. 188.

48 Paul Tillich, *The Protestant Era* (Chicago: Chicago University Press, 1948), p. 112.

49 Jean-François Lyotard, *The Postmodern Condition* (Minneapolis: University of Minnesota Press, 1993), p. xxiv.

50 For more on this, see *McDonaldization of the Church*, pp. 133–54.

51 Cf. Gordon Lynch, *After Religion* (London: Darton, Longman & Todd, 2002).

52 Coupland, *Generation X*, p. 8. This is a recurring theme throughout his writings. At the end of *Life after God*, he confides 'My secret is that I need God. . .'

4

Sacred persons

Timothy Jenkins

In this exploration of what we mean by 'sacred persons', I shall
be concerned with various narrative accounts, told by sociologists, of who we are and how we got to be that way. This is not
a perspective from within a religious or theological discourse,
but a necessarily external, sociological gaze, which requires a
different terminology from that found in other parts of this book
(for example, 'sacramental' becomes 'sacred'). However, the two
approaches have enough in common to allow comparisons to
emerge. Here is a first, short story. In the past, all sorts of things,
institutions, places and people were marked as 'special', in the
sense that they possessed exceptional value or legitimacy, worth
or authority. They were what we may call 'sacred'. In the
modern period, however, this characteristic force or quality has
departed from these different locations. This loss, which may be
celebrated or regretted according to taste, is a way of describing
both the character of modernity and the transition to it: we have
become secularized. A particular problem in this condition is the
loss of charisma experienced by the churches, in the liturgy, and
in the figure of the priest. The quality of being sacred captures
various properties, named as value, worth, legitimacy and
authority. You might notice two things about these terms.[1] First,
they imply relationships between things, persons, institutions
and so forth. We are not dealing with qualities possessed by iso-
lated entities as part of their identity. Rather, we are dealing in

evaluations, based on contrastive differences: this is worth more than that, or has a greater significance than the other, or has power over these specified others, and so on. Second, this evaluative relationship has an inescapably temporal dimension, explored in such terms as credit, debt, promise, obedience, loyalty and so forth. These terms contain both a particular past and a future; they are 'tensed'. They express a relation both of power and commitment. This dimension may be summed up as 'obligation'. Or, we might say, the sacred is connoted by the modal mood; it is marked by relations of 'ought' and 'must'. The disappearance of the sacred may then be defined as the weakening both of relationship and of obligation to others: a loss of differentiation in space and time. Or to put it the other way round, secularization is implied in the rise of the individual, conceived of as equal to any other, and as autonomous. Its rise represents a homogenization of space and time. A sacred person is essentially a representative in whom relations of difference and obligation are condensed, whether we are talking of a priest or a king, a judge or a magician. At first sight, the individual is then the antithesis of such figures. My focus in this paper is on how some sociologists have handled this opposition.

The concept of 'the sacred'

Before pursuing these narratives, I shall offer some brief observations on the concept of the sacred being employed here, which derives from Durkheim;[2] indeed, most of my examples derive from the history of French sociology. The first thing to say is that we need to separate the idea of the sacred from any notions of experience. This is a crucial distinction to grasp in light of the recourse of several contributions in this volume to aesthetic notions. We are not concerned with any sense of awe, or of mystery, or of the holy, nor are we engaged with encounters with gods, spirits or ancestors. These things certainly exist, but they are not our primary concern, for they refer to categories generated by the notion of the individual: they presume the primacy of the individual psyche or mind. If the key to intelligibility lies in the individual, a certain account of secularization has been accepted in advance – and the sociologist's task becomes that of explaining how people once held views that gave the illusion of relatedness and obligation. Durkheim's counter-claim runs along the lines that humans exist primarily in groups, and that groups elaborate and organize themselves through systems of evaluation and obligation. He calls these systems of shared discrimination 'collective representations', which he saw as the product of the ratiocination of many minds, contained in what he called 'institutions'. Collective representations are both richer in content and different from the product of the individual mind; they represent the resources that every person puts to use. For everybody thinks and uses their imagination only by using the products of previous human intelligence transmitted to them. The ultimate source of the authority with which we are concerned comes from this collective intelligence. The intuitive example of such an institution is human language: it is transmitted and taught without reflection; it contains specific traditions and forms of understanding. And yet it is simultaneously the means for initiative and exploration, the results of which may be shared, evaluated and passed on. The notion of collective representations simultaneously permits the idea of individual vocations and makes sense of social organizations, including their consecration of callings as they endorse representatives or sacred persons. It also allows us to grasp why things, persons or places gain their sacred properties only under certain conditions and for certain times: it contains a sociological account of the sacramental. It is worth remarking that the scale of these representations, organizing classifications and distributing values need not be large. Meaning is produced by quite small and discrete collections of humans with their own memories, practices and possibilities – such as churches. Human being is constructed above the individual level and below the universal, at an intermediate scale.

We might sum up Durkheim's account of the sacred by making the following point: the opposition of sacred to profane concerns not two classes of things in the world – things which are holy, things which are not – so much as the uneven distribution of value among things. The world is made up of profane facts but sometimes, in the course of inspecting them, a particular fact will cause you to think, and this is because you have encountered an anomaly that is a pointer to a higher logical level of classification or ordering. Anomalies mark boundaries; if you cross a boundary, you will experience the force of the collective mind, embodied in its institutions. Let me give a simple example. In Britain you may get married at any age you like, and there is a statistical distribution of the age at which people get married. However this field of possibilities is created by a prescription: you cannot get married under the age of sixteen. This boundary is well marked by custom, morality and the law. The profane fact of marriage choices is constructed by a fact of a completely different sort. You could not tell in advance, for sixteen is simply one number in a sequence, without any natural or divine significance. Yet if you cross that boundary, you will experience the force of the collective mind, embodied in its institutions. In this account the absolute distinction between sacred and profane is that between prescription and preference, a difference of logical level.[3] In such a perspective, institutions pay attention to the sacred, iterating and reiterating its conditions. Sacred persons are representatives of such institutions, embodying and relating to their powers of definition, tending the particular compulsions which are the institutions' concern. And sacraments express these definitional forces at their most intense. All this is normally taken for granted; we are blinded by habit to the exceptional nature of these forces. It takes a particular occasion to draw our attention to the arbitrary but real energies at work, a challenge to the categories which we register generally as a threat. Yet these challenges are continually generated, because collective ratiocination is ceaseless. We are the authors of our own collective uneasiness and, at times, precipitate crises.

The 'loss' of the sacred

This uneasiness lies at the root of sociology as a discipline. One way of telling its story is to say that sociology began as a lament for the loss of the sacred. In France, in particular, sociology emerged as a way of making sense of the unprecedented experience of the Revolution and its consequences. And the Revolution was conceived as an abrupt transition from tradition to modernity, as a crisis at a fundamental level in the order of life. Indeed one initial explanatory metaphor employed to describe the change was 'divorce' – as in Louis de Bonald's pamphlet of 1800, 'Concerning Divorce', which may be the first study of the sociology of the family.[4] The primary locus of divorce is between wife and husband, but the metaphor is extended to cover the breakdown of relations between parents and children, between employer and employees, between the king and his subjects, between the Church and the people, even between God and man. Divorce describes a crisis in every sphere: sexual, family, economic, political and religious. And what is being lost in this account is the sacred, or authority in all its forms: legitimacy, worth, sovereignty and charisma are all being contested and destroyed. The initial description of modernity as secularization then is as de-sacralizing: a loss of particularity and differentiation on the one hand and of forms of belonging together on the other. Modernity is defined negatively as a loss of the possibility of being someone in relation to others, of belonging to particular common projects, and of joining in something that gives meaning and purpose. The modern human experience is one of existential loss, of disorder, disorientation and isolation. It is in this period that the term *anomie* emerges, and suicide becomes a sociological topic.[5] It is worth remarking that humans tend to map out the experience of change in the most basic terms available to them, expressing it in terms of marriage and kinship and their breakdown. Kinship and alliance, or those solidarities you cannot avoid and those that you choose, are bound to be used as basic metaphors for human relations and their disruption. So the notion of divorce, or describing social relations in terms of the disruption of the relation between the sexes, is important, and recurs.[6]

61

Political solution – a conservative perspective

Various political options emerged out of this initial analysis, each concerned to adapt social relations – a new concept[7] – in order to create better human lives. Moreover, sacred persons feature in each of these approaches, as a key to the solution. The most extreme and the earliest response looked to the possibility of restoring hierarchy and order. This approach is best exemplified by de Maistre,[8] who speaks of the need for an irrational principle of authority to be reimposed by force on society. One cannot reason for the sacred; it must be made to happen. He looked therefore to the recreation of the roles of the sacred King and the Pope, of priests and fathers and, above all, of the public executioner. The Catholic Church kept its distance from such speculations. This conservative strand has had some startling progeny; one might look, for example, to Carl Schmitt's critique of Liberalism in the 1930s, which continues to play a role in contemporary foreign policy debates under the term 'exceptionalism'.[9] This strand of the story raises the question of the place of wickedness in the history we are considering: a sociology of the sacred, and a theology of the sacramental, may find themselves allied to or appealed to by an 'irrational' politics of the right. At present, I have no answers to offer to this problem.

Political solution – a social reform perspective

There were subsequent, less extreme discussions for social reform, putting forward reasoned proposals to overcome the dissolution effected by modern individualism without retreating to *ancien régime*-style patriarchy. Le Play was an important figure, now neglected, whose work was taken up by Catholic social reformers and by *Action Française*. The aim was to provide the means to restore social cohesion in the form of hierarchy, right order, and continuity, whilst simultaneously creating citizens for modern society. At issue were the appropriate forms of authority, legitimacy, worth and so forth that respond to the demands of the modern world. The means chosen focused on reforming the laws of inheritance. The restoration of the untrammelled right of the owner of property to leave it as he willed was supposed to restore paternal authority, preserve businesses intact over generations through single inheritance, and thereby provide means and motivation for intergenerational solidarity and care. In this process, the sacred persons are the father and the heir, in whom the family is represented and legitimacy resides. They are crucial to creating continuity, while at the same time non-heirs are generated as (conservative) citizens, fit for modern society and yet rooted in an ongoing household.

Starting with reform of the family, new patterns of economic and political life were to be evolved, the overall issue being to adapt civil society to the modern context. These settlements were to be consecrated by religion. Despite their unfashionableness, these concerns, too, endure to the present; they are not absent from either national or European Community policies. We are still searching for means of distributing and sustaining value within human networks and relations.

A reappraisal of 'individualism'

Both conservatives and social reformers were aiming to restore the sacred by the manipulation of social relations. Their principal target was the individual, and their argument was as follows. In the place of social solidarities endorsed by tradition, post-Revolutionary society had substituted the rights of the individual backed by the sophistries of reason (the philosophers). It is because of individualism that wives divorce their husbands, children rebel against their parents, employees owe no duty to the owners of businesses, the people reject first their king and then serially their political masters, and humankind has no need of God or of his priests. The rise of the individual is perceived as the end of the sacred, as egoism and desire replace solidarity and duty.[10] Yet not every writer accepted such an account. Durkheim suggested that these accounts did not contain a sociological analysis but instead projected an actor's account of the experience of the nineteenth century.[11] It cannot be the case that the sacred is

63

lost, for, as long as there is social order, there will be evaluation
in the form of collective orderings of desire and obligation.[12]
How then are we to describe individualism? Individualism
cannot be precisely true in the terms of its own claims, for if we
were all truly autonomous individuals, the idea of individualism
would have occurred only to one or two inspired visionaries
capable of great insight.[13] As it is, individualism is held by all as a
part of common sense. It is a universal truth. It is therefore a
morality, a collective representation by means of which modern
social groups order themselves and describe their identity. Like all
moral facts it has its negative side. We experience that negative in
the potential for isolation and loss of direction present in our
society, and in such aspects as a collective loss of vision and taste.
We live, Durkheim says, in an age of moral mediocrity.[14] We may
reflect, too, upon the responsibilities of economic and political
institutions that interact with and promote individualism in such
a world: the dynamics of commercial interest and the nature of
democracy. At the same time it is worth remarking on the relo-
cation of the sacred in such a morality: the person has become
sacred. Everyman is his or her own representative, priest and
king, legislator and judge. One of the marks of a collective representation is that this claim carries absolute conviction. Even as
critics we are sovereign and rely on our own authority. We cannot
imagine – except as a fiction – a state in which we would
acknowledge other modalities of authority. If we are seeking then
the whereabouts of sacred persons in our world, they are not to
be found in the big men of representative democracy, or in busi-
ness leaders, or in the celebrities generated by media commercial
interests. Although each of these attractive figures has a fascina-
tion, they lack precisely the unquestioned authority, legitimacy
and so forth of the sacred person. This certainty does however
inhere in the sovereignty of the individual.

Individualism as a 'social fact'

Let us then explore some aspects of the individual, considered as
a collective representation. First, the sovereignty of the individual

is a curious historical construct, a compound of the right of resistance, taken as a sign of God's Spirit, and an inversion of the divine right of kings. In the period of the English Revolution, defenders of the king's authority borrowed the Continental theory of absolute sovereignty; this was not a description of a previously existing state of affairs, but an ideological weapon forged for battle. It was adopted by the opponents of royal power and applied to the emergent individual, in the claim that every person is a divine king with absolute right of disposal of the objects in his sway. This power included rights over other persons to the extent that their rights were not infringed. And this politically defined figure was readily adopted in the Revolutionary period in France, where a sacred king was likewise slain, and it emerges in the early accounts of social relations.[15] A thoroughly sacred creature therefore underlies the banalities of *homo oeconomicus* and rational choice theory and is endlessly repeated in accounts of secularization. And because it is sacred, the individual cannot readily be grasped, but rather causes us to think. The individual is not an ontological entity, but is constituted by a series of exclusions; it is the effect of higher order prescriptions, and as such bears in it the marks of what it is not. So whilst appearing to be the end-point of a process, the figure is better understood in terms of the process itself, for it contains incompatible opposites. In it we experience an endlessly repeated movement from collective solidarities to personal responsibility, expressed in ecclesial perspectives in such forms as the shift from ritual to integrity, from High Church to Low, from a world of faith to a secular world, and so forth. The sacramental is experienced largely in its denial, a felt absence. Individualism is the product of a collective representation which has effects in the world, but it is not an adequate description of that world. This reiterates the point that, while individual psychology or mind is not a sufficient basis to explain social facts, the persuasiveness of the recourse to psychology is an indicator of the power of the representation of individualism. And just as social actors take their understanding of the world as the truth of their situation, rather than as an orientation to help them cope with it, so sociologists tend to project a persuasive interpretation of the world as the key to understanding it, rather than perceiving that the world is in large part made up from such interpretations and their interactions.

In sum, individualism is not an exhaustive account of the world, even though it is an important component, especially because of its virtual monopoly over the terms of public debate. And we might conclude that while secularization is an important concept, it too is difficult to define. Once we have grasped that, so long as they live in groups, humans will secrete value as they classify, order and evaluate, the issue becomes recast. Rather than meaning evaporating from the world, the sacred 'deterritorializes' and 'reterritorializes'.[16] Part of the interest of the concept of collective representations is that it points to a certain openness with respect to the new, both an adaptation to what is the case, and the ability through acts of intelligence and imagination to contribute in novel ways. It is possible to participate in the new on the basis of the old, through definition, observation and explanation. This is how small groups contribute to the life of larger ones, which share in the interpretations as they test them out and adapt them. We might add, in this light, that the task of religion – of the Church – has always been to pay attention to the forms of life in society, both to promote the aspirations to human flourishing they contain, and to criticize them from the basis of what is already understood. Religion concerns the purging of idolatry and the purification of desire.[17] In this account, religion has no fixed content to be transmitted despite the world, but is always construing the new on the basis of the old. This gives it its characteristic tension between tradition and syncretism. It also allows us to see why the forms of religion are never pure or self-referential, but always have to adapt or die. And it is worth observing that even the most conservative forms represent a continual energetic process of re-imagining: forms of life without life in them rapidly turn to dust.

A contemporary challenge

These features challenge sociologists who, in common with most human activity, try to predict the new on the basis of the old, as somehow contained in it. They usually monitor change as decline; statistics in particular lend themselves to measuring alteration from a defined state.[18] On these grounds, I distrust most accounts of the present and near future, however skilled.[19] Also for this kind of reason, sociologists are rather slow in grasping the significance of contemporary movements. In the late 1980s and 1990s there were two large-scale social movements, neither of which was anticipated by sociologists. The first was the fall of Communism, the second the rise of charismatic Christianity as a global phenomenon. These two failures are sufficiently striking to demand an explanation, which would lie in the area I have indicated: sociology constitutes a perspective that eliminates a priori all signs of the sacred as a condition of modernity, and therefore cannot account for new compelling forms of social behaviour. One effect of such a perspective is to eliminate from the subjects of sociology any capacity for intelligence and self-imagining. Secularization theory at this level is a failure of imagination on the part of the sociological mind, which articulates the deterritorialization and reterritorialization of the forms of social energy in a story of the loss of trust, polity, legitimacy and so forth, whilst being inevitably surprised by the unexpected return of the repressed. The task for the sociologist should rather be to describe both the inevitable experiences of loss and to detect where life, in the form of compulsions ordering the social, is emerging. The value to us of the belated interest shown in charismatic Christianity is then that it provides a case study of the reterritorialization of the sacred, an account of the return of moral order to set alongside those accounts of the demoralization of the world.[20] It also upsets some of our liberal theological pieties in a way that may cause us to think (a sure sign of the presence of the sacred).

Pentecostal Christianity

The sociological thesis is, broadly speaking, that Pentecostal Christianity plays the role of allowing the poor and not-so-poor of the developing world to adapt to economic, social and cultural change. Just as in earlier Protestant phases, religion creates the possibility of order and meaning within the chaos and dislocation of modernity. It does so by giving resources of hope and healing, integration and community, and teaching skills such as literacy and responsibility, focused in the conversion of a person to Christ. Conversion and belonging to the communities of the converted together create a socially empowered individual capable of coping with problems and of grasping possibilities in this new and fragmented world. There are millions of such people in Latin America, the Caribbean, throughout Africa, in the Far East, in the ruins of the old Communist bloc, and among immigrants from these areas to the West. Amongst the features of this 'movement', it is particularly significant that the family is a central focus of the renewed way of life. Women especially are favoured with spiritual gifts, as healers and prophets; they are slain in the spirit, receive tongues and are inspired to prayer. Above all, as Bernice Martin – whose account I am following – says: 'women have used the Pentecostal religious discourse to rewrite the moral mandate on which sexual relations and family life rest'.[21] The collective needs of the household unit are put above the freedom and pleasures of men, and this revaluation is sanctioned and endorsed by the church community. This re-negotiation of the settlement between the sexes is generally not remarked on in studies of the resources Protestant Christianity supplies, and yet it responds directly to the metaphor of divorce that lies at the heart of modernity. It seeks to restore relations between men and women and between parents and children, and to use this restoration as the basis for establishing new possibilities in the spheres of employment, politics and religion. It is a response to modernity: social reform from below. Martin spells out why this movement, and its gender-related nature, has largely been missed by social scientists. Sociologists of religion have focused on secularization and new religious movements, and missed a revival of conservative Christianity. Marxists and others (Liberationists, for example) have been determined to see the movement as evidence of United States imperialism, and not as of indigenous origin. Feminists looking for the defeat of patriarchy have not grasped this unexpected way that women are renegotiating the forms of their lives. None of these intellectual traditions is content with a movement of self-improvement that creates new possibilities of human flourishing by strengthening and defining gender roles, promoting strong religious values, and seeking to join in the opportunities Capitalism offers. None of the forms of these negotiations responds precisely to our agenda for reform. Nor are their sacred persons quite ours: for example, male leaders and pastors endorsed by their congregations, but with wider political and economic interests, and within congregations, 'good wives' and 'independent women', who embody the values of faith, family and engagement in the world of work. This movement has not had much purchase at present in the West. But it has an interest, beyond being an episode in sociological history, in that it offers a potential resource which, because of the adaptive power of human minds and imaginations, may be taken up in some new form. In some fundamental ways, we conceive the ills of our society in terms of the breakdown of ties of kinship and alliance. In the Church this takes the more direct form, that many of the most contentious issues are articulated around topics of sexuality, whether concerned with the expression of desire, gender relations, or the division of labour. So a movement that puts the force of the Holy Spirit into a redefinition of the settlement between the sexes and reformulating the bases of family life could speak to our condition. This is speculation: the Spirit – or the Sacred – moves where it will. But notice that if social energies are renewed along these lines, intellectuals of all kinds will be wrong-footed. Reorganization of value will take place as it were beneath the conscious categories. We will not imitate, but create; my only suggestion is that sexual difference may play a countervailing role to the equality of individuals. For, just as individualism is not a true description of the world, but an orientation that allows people to act in the world, so the liberal agenda cannot be carried to fruition.

Conclusion

How best to sum up what I have said? First, the sacred does not die away, but shifts. This is not necessarily comforting; it does not mean, for example, that the Christian faith must continue. Rather, history repeatedly takes unexpected forms. Second, individualism is a complex moral mapping, in which the disappearance of familiar solidarities and their replacement by atomized desires is endlessly repeated. It is a powerful shared account of the world that is neither true nor untrue.

Third, sacred persons are created by collective representations; they are the products of an immense labour of intelligence, imagination, and collective ratiocination. As such, they are double, in the sense discussed earlier of being dependent and mutable, whilst also possessing authority and a sense of insistence or permanence. Fourth, the forms such persons will take can be imagined but not anticipated.

Notes

1 They bear comparison with Begbie's remarks on the elementary characteristics of musical notes. See pp. 173–91.

2 The classic exposition is Émile Durkheim (trans. Joseph Swain 1915), *The Elementary Forms of the Religious Life* (London: HarperCollins, repr. 1976), ch. 1, originally published as É. Durkheim, *Les formes élémentaires de la vie religieuse: le système totémique en Australie* (Paris, 1912).

3 See Claude Lévi-Strauss, *The Elementary Structures of Kinship* (Boston, MA: Beacon Press, 1992), originally published as *Les structures élémentaires de la parenté* (Paris, 1949).

4 See chapter on 'Conservatism and Sociology', in Robert Nisbet, *Tradition and Revolt* (New York: Random House, 1968), for an account of the conservative sources at the origin of French sociology, and John Milbank, *Theology and Social Theory* (Oxford: Blackwell, 1990) for a differing interpretation.

5 See Louis de Bonald, *Du divorce* (Paris, 1900), p. 176; P. Lammenais, *Oeuvres complètes* (Brussels, 1839), II: pp. 150–1, and Émile Durkheim, *Le Suicide: étude de sociologie* (Paris, 1897), English trans., *Suicide* (London: Routledge, 1992).

6 A recent example is Callum Brown, *The Death of Christian Britain* (London and New York: Routledge, 2000).

7 See Pierre Macherey, 'Aux sources des "rapports sociaux" – Bonald, St. Simon, Guizot', in *Genèses* 9 (1992), pp. 25–42.

8 Joseph de Maistre, 'Premier entretien', in Richard Lebrun (ed.), *St. Petersburg Dialogues,* trans. of original of 1821, (Montreal: McGill-Queen's University Press, 1993); cf. Roger Caillois, 'Sociologie du bourreau' (1939) in Denis Hollier (ed.), *Le collège de sociologie* (Paris, 1979), English trans., D. Hollier (ed.), *The College of Sociology: 1937–1939* (Minneapolis, MN: University of Minnesota Press, 1988).

9 Carl Schmitt, *The Concept of the Political* (Chicago: University of Chicago Press, 1996, trans. of original of 1932).

10 We may compare this account with Weber's description of the framework, within which the only possible response to technological rationalism, which lacks any *telos* except efficiency, is a romanticism whereby human response gives arbitrary value to one aspect or another of the process – see Max Weber, 'Science as a vocation' (1919) and 'Politics as a vocation' (1919), in H. H. Gerth and C. Wright Mills (eds & trans), *From Max Weber: Essays in Sociology* (London and New York: Routledge, 1998); Max Weber, *The Protestant Ethic and the Spirit of Capitalism* (Oxford: Blackwell, 2001), trans. of original first published in 1905. It is debatable whether aesthetic accounts of the sacramental escape from this iron cage thesis.

11 See his comments on Frédéric Le Play, *La Réforme sociale en France, déduite de l'observation comparée des peuples européens* (Paris, 1864), in Émile Durkheim, *Les règles de la méthode sociologique* (Paris, 1895), English trans., É. Durkheim, *The Rules of Sociological Method* (London: Macmillan 1992).

12 Émile Durkheim, *Sociology and Philosophy* (New York: Macmillan, 1982), originally published as *Sociologie et philosophie* (Paris, 1924).

13 Émile Durkheim, 'L'individualisme et les intellectuels', *Revue Bleue,* 4e série, X (1898), pp. 7–13.

14 Durkheim, *The Elementary Forms of the Religious Life*, p. 427. (See note 2 above.)

15 It would be a task to establish this genealogy. See John Neville Figgis, *The Divine Right of Kings* (Bristol: Thoemmes Press, 1994, original 1896), Alan Macfarlane (on Maitland), *The Making of the*

Modern World (Basingstoke: Palgrave Macmillan, 2002), and Pierre Klossowski (on de Sade), 'Le marquis de Sade et la Révolution' (1939), in Hollier (ed.), *Le collège de sociologie*. (See note 8 above.)

16 To borrow two terms from Gilles Deleuze, *Mille Plateaux* (Paris, 1972).

17 Cf. Nicholas Lash, *The Beginning and the End of Religion* (Cambridge: Cambridge University Press, 1996), p. 70.

18 See Timothy Jenkins, *Religion in English Everyday Life* (Oxford & New York: Berghahn, 1999), pp. 23–39.

19 Take, for example, this judgement by Hervieu-Léger, one of the best current sociologists of religion: 'If, in the future, the authenticity of the personal spiritual journey becomes more important than the conformity of belief demanded of the religious faithful by the institution, the legitimacy of religious authority will be attacked at its very foundation'. Danielle Hervieu-Léger, 'Individualism, the validation of faith, and the social nature of religion in modernity' in Richard Fenn (ed.), *The Blackwell Companion to Sociology of Religion* (Oxford: Blackwell, 2001), pp. 161–75, esp.173. This projects a current experience drawn from a more complex current reality as a future (conditional) state. These correlations might be true, sometimes, under certain conditions – but we would need to know what would count as evidence, and how to evaluate it. The value of such a claim either as a generalization or a prediction is very dubious.

20 See Fenn in *The Blackwell Companion to Sociology of Religion*, p. 7.

21 Bernice Martin 'The Pentecostal gender paradox: a cautionary tale for the sociology of religion' in *The Blackwell Companion to Sociology of Religion*, pp. 52–60, esp. 54; she cites Elisabeth Brusco, *The Reformation of Machismo: Evangelical Conversion and Gender in Colombia* (Texas: University of Texas Press, 1995) as an exemplary ethnography.

5

The image of God and the biblical roots of Christian sacramentality

Crispin H. T. Fletcher-Louis

It has sometimes been said that the purest religion of Israel is fundamentally non-sacramental, if not anti-sacramental,[1] and in this regard the theological and ecclesiological commitments of modern (Christian) biblical scholarship have perhaps dictated the terms on which Scripture is treated. Israel opposed the 'magical' and cultic worldview of its pagan neighbours, just as Protestants have opposed the ritual and 'priestcraft' of Catholic religion. However, recent developments challenge a non-sacramental view of Israelite religion from several fronts. There is now a renewed interest in a comparativist method that recognizes the considerable continuities between the cultic realities of the ancient Near East and the religious life of Israel.[2] The leavening influence of Jewish scholarship is also stimulating a fresh appreciation of the sacrificial and cultic material that dominates the Pentateuch. Commentators are now happier to acknowledge the many ways that, in her worship, her sacrifices and her construction of sacred space and time, Israel shares ancient Near Eastern assumptions about the efficacy of ritual and the need for signs that mediate the divine presence. It is an exciting time to be re-examining the biblical roots of a Christian sacramentalism.[3]

There are many avenues our search could take. In what follows here, I address one particular issue that underlies so much modern, Western and especially Protestant antipathy to the sacramental; that is, an overly negative anthropology which opposes divine and human identities in such a way that, inevitably, the role of humanity in the mediation of divine presence and activity must be downplayed.

If the biblical drama, as conceived by the Church, can be played out in three acts – creation and 'fall'; God's choice of and intimate dealings with his people, Israel; followed by the life of Christ and the Church, his body – then I rehearse here only some of the plot of the first two acts. Although I will reflect briefly on the significance of these in isolation, the way the third act continues and transforms these plotlines would, of course, need full consideration in any thoroughgoing study of the historical and theological shape of the biblical roots of sacramental theology.

The creation of humanity 'as God's image'

What does it mean that, in Genesis 1.26–27, God creates humanity in his image and likeness?[4] It is widely held that here there is a democratization of the language and ideology of ancient Near Eastern kingship: where the king once stood as a god's vicar, now the whole of humanity is his representative. There is some truth in this view since the king in Mesopotamia and Egypt can be viewed as a god's 'image',[5] and, of course, this reading suits a tradition that cherishes a priesthood of all believers to the exclusion of any mediation through a distinct priestly or royal order. But Genesis 1 itself belongs to the P strand of the Pentateuch whose theology is fully articulated in the cultic material in Exodus, Leviticus and Numbers. There, priests stand centre stage mediating God's presence to the rest of Israel from whom they are carefully separated. Considerable time is given to the maintenance of the proper boundaries between priests, Levites and laity (see especially Num. 1.48–54; 4.16–18). It is true that there is no king anywhere in this material, but this is primarily because Moses and the high priest are painted in royal colours. So, neither is there the flat democratization of human privilege that commentators are so fond of finding in Genesis 1.26. Perhaps the 'image' language of Genesis 1.26 has another purpose? A new understanding of the 'image-of-God' language that must be included in any full interpretation has recently appeared. This is that *humanity is created to be the one creator god's cult statue, his idol.* 'Image' language is cult statue or idol language. This is how the word *tselem* is normally used in the Old Testament (for example, Num. 33.52; 1 Sam. 6.5; 11; 2 Kings 11.18) and in a cognate Akkadian expression for an image of (a) god(s) (*tsalam ili/ilani*). For several reasons it must be this meaning which is in mind for the Priestly author of Genesis 1. Other parts of Genesis 1 are a polemic against the polytheism of pagan cosmogonies: the sun, moon and stars are not gods; sea monsters are *created* on the fifth day; there is no violent struggle in the act of creation, and so forth. And the Genesis 1 account of creation has its *Sitz-im-Leben* in the Priestly view of the cult and its liturgy.[6] Therefore, to use language otherwise reserved for idols for humanity at the climax of the account of creation is either dangerously obtuse or deliberately subversive. Deliberate subversion must then be the intention: the Israelite view of the cosmos has at its apex the human being – not the sun, moon, stars, animals or other created realities – as the particular concrete physical form and manifestation of the one creator god. As Mayer Gruber has now pointed out this also explains the otherwise vexing Hebrew *beth* in the phrases 'Let us make *'adam betsalmenu* . . . and God created the *'adam betsalmo, betselem* of God he created him . . .' (Gen. 1.26–27). This is best taken as a *beth pretii* which gives the translation 'And God said, 'Let us make man *in the place* of our image . . . And God created the *'adam in the place of* his statue, *instead of* God's idol he created him. . .'[7] In the words of Herbert Niehr:

> Gen 1:26 . . . can only be understood against the background of an ancient YHWH statue . . . man is regarded as the statue of God. We are told in Gen 1:26f. that man is created according to God's *slm* and *dmwt*. Here the terms *slm* and *dmwt* are used as synonyms denoting

a 'statue'. Humans were thus created to be the living statues of the deity . . . There was no further need of a divine image because . . . humans represented YHWH, as a statue would have done . . .[8]

Over against zoomorphic paganism, Genesis 1 presents anthropomorphic monotheism, with a vision of creation as a well-ordered cultic space in which all the antechambers for lesser gods and their statues have been emptied lest the sight of the creator god in his human 'statue', in the central and highest holy of holies, be obscured. The point here is to give the biblical prohibition of idolatry its strongest possible rationale: for us to make an idol is foolish because it fails to appreciate that, according to the original and intended order of creation, it is humanity which is to function in relation to the one and only creator god as do pagan statues and idols in relation to their gods. Idolatry means emptying our transcendence into that which cannot bear divine immanence.

To appreciate the full force of this image-of-God-in-humanity theology we must have in mind the role of idols in ancient Near Eastern religion. In the religious practice of Israel's neighbours an idol is set up to be the real presence and visible form of the god. Because the god really does inhabit the image, the image *is* the god, and its proper care (clothing, washing, feeding) and veneration guarantees the god's benefits and protection for the worshipping community. The divinized statue has both rights and responsibilities in relation to its community. Without the right worship of the image by the community their social, economic and military welfare is jeopardized. If the statue of a tutelary god is captured by an enemy then that god abandons the community. The role of the god and its statue in the socio-political sphere is mirrored in the cosmological sphere. If the statues of those gods responsible for creation are not properly attended then creation itself is liable to return to chaos. With this understanding of divine images assumed, the Priestly account of creation has a sharply focused theological anthropology: humanity is to be the eyes, ears, mouth, being and action of the creator god within his creation. S. Dean McBride puts the matter provocatively when he says:

. . . this unifying image in humankind has a sacramental as well as an essentially corporeal function: Adamic beings are animate icons . . . the peculiar purpose for their creation is 'theophanic': to represent or mediate the sovereign presence of deity within the central nave of the cosmic temple, just as cult-images were supposed to do in conventional sanctuaries. [This means that humanity is] an inherently ambivalent species whose temporal existence blurs, by design, the otherwise sharp distinction between creator and creation.[9]

Loosely speaking, then, Genesis 1 is an 'incarnational' text.[10] It is humanity that has the peculiar responsibility for bearing divine presence and carrying out the divine will; both of these in a thoroughly physical fashion. In the first instance, the statement 'God became man' exegetes Israel's understanding of the original creation.

Israel's high priest is God's image-idol in the cult-as-microcosm

If humanity is created to be God's idol what happens after 'the fall'? We are usually told that Israel's religion is aniconic; in the cult there is no Yahweh statue. But our reading of Genesis 1 suggests an alternative possibility: that just as humanity functions as God's idol in Genesis 1, so a human being or beings function as cult statues in Israel's worship. Indeed, there are good reasons for thinking that humanity's function as God's image-idol is reconstituted in its most visible and perfect form in Israel's high priesthood at Sinai. As a first step towards an appreciation of this theme we must consider the cosmological identity of Israel's ideal cultic space as it is represented in the Tabernacle. It is now widely acknowledged that Genesis 1 has been composed as a carefully structured parallel to material in Exodus 25–40 where the details of the Tabernacle in the wilderness are revealed to Moses. In Exodus 25–31 Moses is given instructions for the various parts of the Tabernacle in seven speeches, the contents of which in one way or another (in some cases more obvious than others) correspond to the seven days of creation. For example, in the third speech Moses is told to make a bronze laver (30.17–21) otherwise called 'the sea' (1 Kings 7.39), just as God created the sea (and the dry land) on the third day of creation. In Exodus 40 (vv. 16–33), as Margaret Barker in particular has shown, the stages of the setting up of the Tabernacle correspond to the seven days of creation.[11] Furthermore the climax to the construction of the Tabernacle echoes the climax of creation, as if to say, in this cultic world creation is restored or completed:

Gen. 2.1 Thus the heavens and the earth were finished (Heb. *yekullu*, Gk *sunetelesthesan*), and all their multitude (*ho kosmos auton*).	Exod. 39.32a In this way all the work of the tabernacle of the tent of meeting was finished (*tekel*).
Gen. 2.2 And on the seventh day God finished (*yekal*, *sunetelesen*) the work (*mela'kto, ta erga autou*) that he had done, and he rested on the seventh day from all the work that he had done.	Exod. 40.33 He set up the court around the tabernacle and the altar . . . So Moses finished the work (*yekal . . . hammela'kah, sunetelesen . . . ta erga*).

The parallels between the conclusion to the creation account and the conclusion to the preparation of the Tabernacle mean that what Moses does for the latter is in imitation of, or an extension of, God's work in creation. The same point is made through the theme of blessing in the two parts of P's work:

Gen. 1.28 God *blessed* them (man and woman) (*yebarek 'otam, eulogesen autous*) . . . Gen. 2.3 So God blessed (*yebarek, eulogesen*) the seventh day and hallowed it . . .	Exod. 39.43 [LXX v. 23] When Moses saw that they had done all the work (*kol hammela'kah, panta ta erga*) just as the LORD had commanded, he blessed them (*yebarek 'otam, eulogesen autous*).

Exodus 39.43 is the only act of blessing in the whole of Exodus 25–40 and it is comprehensively ambivalent: Moses blesses both the people and their works. Moses' blessing thus recapitulates

God's original blessing of both humanity and his works, especially the Sabbath. This is a brief discussion of a complex intratextuality between creation and Tabernacle. The point of the intratextuality is to claim that the cult is a microcosm, and this means that Genesis 1 creates the expectation – I would argue – that within the cult-as-microcosm we will find an image, or idol, of the creator. Indeed, this is precisely how Aaron, Israel's high priest, enters the stage: In Israel's Tabernacle (and Temple) the role of the cult statue is played by the high priest who is the visible and concrete image of the creator within the temple-as-microcosm. Briefly, this point can be seen through a few interpretative observations.

Aaron's garments are the Israelite version of the golden garments of the gods

The apparatus of high priestly office and the rites of Aaron's ordination dominate Exodus 25–40. Exodus chapter 28 provides a detailed account of Aaron's garments: (the ephod, breastpiece, sash, and so forth), and their materials (gold, blue, purple, crimson yarns, and twelve precious stones – onyx, carnelian, chrysolite and emerald, and so on). And his ordination follows in chapter 29. The idols of the Levant, Mesopotamia and Egypt are typically dressed in glorious, multi-coloured, gold- and jewel-studded garments. The dressing of the garments at the statues' consecration, and regularly thereafter, is an essential feature of their care and veneration. A cult statue is its god when it is properly attired,[12] and the design of Aaron's clothing follows closely the sartorial conventions for ancient idol worship. Although the twelve stones of the breastpiece and the two onyx stones of the shoulders have their own specific symbolic significance, they are a component part, along with the fabrics in gold, blue, purple and crimson, of Israel's version of the golden jewel-studded garments of the gods convention. We can usefully compare, for example, extracts from the following account of the making (or repair) of a cult statue by the seventh-century Assyrian king Esarhaddon:[13]

79

(9) I, Esarhaddon, king of the universe, king of the Land of Ashur, . . . (10) . . . with the great intelligence and vast understanding, (11) which the great Nudimmud, the wise man of the gods, bestowed on me, (12) with the wisdom which Ashur and Marduk entrusted to me . . . (set about restoring the cult statues and prayed to the gods:) . . . (17) may what you yourselves have in your heart be brought about in accordance with your unalterable word. (18) Endow the skilled craftsmen . . . with as high an understanding as Ea, their creator. (19) Teach them skills by your exalted word; (20) make all their handiwork succeed through the craft of Ninshiku . . . . . . (29) I brought carpenters, goldsmiths, metalworkers, stonecutters, 'skilled artisans knowledgeable in the mysteries' into the temple which Shamash and Adad had indicated through divination. (30) I installed the craftsmen there. Red gold, mined in the mountains, which no one had as yet worked for artistic purposes, countless precious stones, (31) not yet cut . .. upon which Ea had generously bestowed his splendour so that they might be fit for the lordly deities, (32) I prepared in abundance for the shrines of the great gods, my lords, and for the bejewelling of their divinity. (33) I gave (all these costly materials) into the pure hands (of the craftsmen). I had made a crown of red gold and precious stones the symbol of the lordship of my lord Ashur, king of the gods; then I returned it to its (proper) place. This crown, clad in awe, (34) full of dignity, bearing brilliance, covered with light, greatly pleased Ashur, the great lord, so that his heart was content and his face gleamed. (35) Bel, Beltiyya, Belet-Babili, Ea, Madanu, the great gods, were ceremoniously borne within the Esharra, the temple of their father (Ashur); (36) and their appearance was beautiful. With red *sariru*-gold, the product of Arallu, ore from the mountains, I decorated their images, (37) With splendid ornaments and precious jewelry I adorned their necks and filled their breasts, exactly as the great lord Marduk wanted and as pleased queen Sarpanitu. (38) They (the artisans) made the statues of their great divinity even more artistic than before. They made them extremely beautiful, and they provided them with an awe-inspiring force, and they made them shine like the sun.

Esarhaddon adorns his idols in the same way that Moses is to adorn Aaron: with gold and precious stones.[14] The Mesopotamian gods thereby carry the splendour of the god Ea (line 31), and the luminous brilliance of the sun, the god Shamash (line 38). So also, the introduction and conclusion that form an *inclusio* around the description of Aaron's garments say they are to be made 'for Glory and for beauty' (Exod. 28.2, 40). With the 'splendid ornaments and precious jewelry' that clothe the gods Esarhaddon specifically 'adorned their necks and filled their breasts' (line 37). Here, too, the language recalls Aaron's garb. Moses is told to 'fill' the breast-piece with a setting (lit. 'a filling *(millu'at)*' of twelve precious stones (Exod. 28.17). For their task the Assyrian king and his craftsmen must possess the wisdom, skill and intelligence of the gods; their craft is endowed with the gods' creative power and intellect (lines 10, 18–19, 29). In Exodus 28, too, those who make Aaron's garments are to 'be wise hearted', and 'filled with the spirit of wisdom' (v. 3). Their leader, we are told a little later, in Exodus 31.2, is Bezalel, whom God has 'filled with the spirit of wisdom and understanding and with knowledge in every kind of craft'. So, Exodus 28 claims that Aaron is the true cultic image-idol: his garments of gold, blue, purple (and crimson and fine linen) are crafted by those who truly have wisdom, under-standing and the spirit of God – the god who created the universe as it is now manifest in the tabernacle-as-microcosm.

What is especially true of the high priest is more generally the case for all priests. In Israel's polemic against idolatry a constant refrain derides the idols of the nations as insensate and immo-bile: the idols have neither eyes that really see, nor ears that really hear, no mouth to speak, no legs with which to walk, and so on (e.g. Isa. 44.18; Jer. 10.5; Ps. 115.4–7). It is against this back-ground that we should read the legal ruling in Leviticus 21.18–20 that no one can serve as priest with a blemish; 'no one who is blind or lame or has a mutilated face or a limb too long, or one who has a broken foot or a broken hand, or a hunchback, or a dwarf, or a man with a blemish in his eyes'. Whatever we make of the justice of these regulations by today's standards, they make perfect sense as a proclamation to Israel's pagan neighbours that here, in Israel's priesthood, are true images of the living god. That Israel's priesthood is the image of the *creator* god can be seen in several of the details of the account in Exodus.

The creation of light and Aaron's tending of the Menorah

We noted above the seven speeches of Exodus 25–31 that correspond to the seven days of creation in Genesis 1. For the first speech to Moses (Exod. 25.1–30.10) P makes a connection between Aaron's tending the temple lampstand and God's creation of light on the first day of creation (Gen. 1.3–5). There are two references to Aaron's responsibilities for the Menorah (27.20–21 and 30.7–8). These make an *inclusio* around the account of Aaron's garments (ch. 28) and his ordination (ch. 29). So, by this *inclusio* the priestly author says that just as 'God brought forth light into darkness (Gen. 1.2–3) so Aaron causes light to shine throughout the night'.[15] In both these instances the menorah is to be tended in the 'evening' and the 'morning' – at the Tamid sacrifice – and so this cultic action marks the primal boundary that results from the creation of light on the first day of creation: God's original creation of light is recapitulated by the priest, in the cult-as-microcosm. The high priest plays the role of the creator on the cultic stage. This is but the tip of a large iceberg. Unfortunately, much of the text's import lies beneath the surface and would take us longer to recover than space here permits. Several points, however, further illustrate the *ways* in which the priesthood functions as God's presence:

The high priest and the mediation of the forgiveness of sins

If the high priest is God's very own presence, it follows that he is able to forgive or take away sins. In Exodus 28.36–38, at the end of the account of Aaron's garments, God commands Moses:

(36) You shall make a rosette of pure gold and you shall engrave on it the engravings of a seal 'holy to Yahweh' (or, 'and you shall engrave on it the engravings of a holy seal 'YHWH''). (37) You shall

fasten it to a blue-purple cord that it may be on the turban, on the front of the turban. (38) It shall be on Aaron's forehead and Aaron shall 'forgive' (or 'bear', 'remove': *naśa'*, *exarei*) the guilt of the holy things that the sons of Israel sanctify for all their holy donations . . .

When Yahweh is the subject of the verb *naśa'* and the object is human sin he *forgives* those sins (e.g., Mic. 7.18; Job 7.21). As Margaret Barker has pointed out, because the high priest is identified with Yahweh through the bearing of his name, what he does in the cult corresponds to what Yahweh himself does in other biblical texts, though how this works is unclear.[16]

The high priest as divine warrior

Israel's god is a warrior. He is the god of the storm; of thunder and lightning, dark clouds and fire. As Margaret Barker and I have tried to show, the high priest is dressed and acts as this divine warrior. For example, according to Josephus, the pomegranates and golden bells at the bottom of his robes (Exod. 28.33–34) symbolize thunder and lightning (*Ant.* 3.184; *B.J.* 5.231) and the sash that hangs at his side represents a serpent; a conquered and tamed Leviathan (*Ant.* 3.154–6).[17] And his exit from the sanctuary (that represents heaven) to the Temple's forecourt (that represents earth) echoes the coming of the divine warrior from heaven to earth.[18] In several early Jewish (pre-Christian) texts the sacramental power of the high priest's embodiment of the divine warrior is assumed. So, for example, in the Qumran *War Scroll* (1QM) that describes the liturgical conduct of the eschatological war between the sons of light and the sons of darkness, the destruction of the forces of darkness by Israel's warriors (on earth) is empowered by the liturgy for which the priests are responsible in the sanctuary (in heaven). The sanctuary's function as microcosm facilitates the mediation of divine power from heaven to earth, and the fulfilment of the Tamid sacrifice, which marks the boundary between light and darkness, energizes the sons of light in their defeat of the sons of darkness.[19]

Priesthood and laity

If Aaron, dressed in all his finery, is the peculiar embodiment of God's presence, mediating forgiveness and divine power, how does his identity relate to that of other Israelites? The *'adam* of Genesis 1 is a figure of universal significance; Aaron is a particular individual. How is the *particular* — Israel's high priest — related to the biblical vision of a *universal* divine presence in the humanity that is God's image? On his breastpiece and lapels the high priest carries the names of the twelve tribes of Israel, and, through the high priest who embodies the nation, Israel — the true humanity in the making — participates in his transcendence. Again, briefly, here are several illustrative observations:

The high priest's garments and the tassels of the ordinary Israelite

It is, of course, true that ordinary Israelites are not dressed as Aaron is dressed. However, in Numbers 15.37–41 all Israelites are told that they must wear 'tassels' (*tsitsit*) containing 'blue–purple cord' (*petil tekelet*) on the hem of their garments. The language in the Hebrew is carefully chosen. It is used elsewhere only in connection with the flower — the rosette (*tsits*) — that carries the name of Israel's god, that is attached to a blue–purple cord (*petil tekelet*), and then to Aaron's forehead (Exod. 28.36). The Old Testament prohibits the combining of wool and linen in clothing (Lev. 19.19; Deut. 22.11). However, whilst this regulation applies for lay Israelites' ordinary clothing, both the high priest's garb and the tassels of Numbers 15.37–41 must be made of this mixed material — dyed wool and linen.[20] So, this 'mixture' of kinds is only possible — and, indeed, is in fact *mandatory* — inasmuch as Israelites share the divine ontology of Israel's priesthood.

Moses and Bezalel

We have already seen ways in which Moses recapitulates God's original act of creation in erecting the Tabernacle. Though a Levite, and therefore ineligible to hold high priestly office, Moses participates in the divine life in other ways. For six days he is with the theophanic cloud on the mountain that penetrates heaven, and on the seventh is taken up into the cloud for a further forty days and nights, during which time he receives instructions for the building of the tabernacle-as-microcosm (Exod. 24.15–18). He is, then, a mystagogue who has been initiated into the divine life and the primordial rhythm and structure of world-forming creativity; the seven-day week. It is entirely fitting that it is the seventh day when Moses enters a full communion with God and his glorious cloud. The command that all Israelites keep the Sabbath is a command that they participate in the divine life. This is the kind of rest that in Mesopotamia is the privilege of the gods, for whom human beings were created as slaves. In Israel, since humanity is God's image, they, like him, are entitled to rest. Not surprisingly, when he descends from the mountain for the last time, in Exodus 34.29ff., Moses is deified with the radiant horns which in the conventions of ancient Near Eastern iconography distinguish gods from mortals. Moses' deification is a degree above that of his contemporaries, even whilst his Sabbatical experience is exemplary for all Israelites. The laity are more straightforwardly presented, in P's system of symbols, by the Judahite Bezalel (from the southern tribes) and his Danite assistant Oholiab (from the northern tribes) (Exod. 31.1–3). Bezalel is 'filled with the spirit of God,' to design and make the Tabernacle and its appurtenances (Exod. 31.2). What Bezalel creates is coterminous with God's own creation of the heavens and the earth and so it is fitting that he is possessed of the same *ruach 'elohim* that hovered over the deep at the dawn of creation (Gen. 1.2). Moreover, all who are similarly skilled, irrespective of tribal qualification, join Bezalel and Oholiab in the work of the Tabernacle (Exod. 35.10; 36.1), since they too possess something of God's image.

Concluding reflections on Israel's image-of-God theology

In view of this kind of material there are both firm conclusions for the biblical roots of sacramental theology and many questions

THE GESTURES OF GOD

that require fuller reflection and study. Two conclusions follow. First, and foremost, this Priestly material – that stands at the canonical heart of the Old Testament – challenges a thoroughgoing anthropological pessimism that would deny or minimize the role of human persons in divine activity. In the 'original' order of creation divine action and being are united in humanity-as-God's-image, just as the presence and action of pagan gods are united in their statues. And, long before *the* Incarnation in Jesus of Nazareth, Israel and her leaders are called to recapitulate that Adamic identity through imitation of, and participation in, God's creativity. The story of the Incarnation begins in Genesis 1 and is already well underway before the Gospels and the life of the Church, Christ's body. Even if the third act of the biblical drama entails some surprising new forms of sacramental and incarnational presence, they cannot be understood apart from a particular theological anthropology and God's purpose in choosing Israel. Second, the well-known Israelite critique of idolatry has regularly been taken as warrant for an iconoclasm that attenuates or denies outright a sacramental spirituality. There can be no denying that this critique is central to Old Testament theology and is assumed in the New Testament. But our new understanding of humanity's role as God's image, and its role in the anti-idolatry polemic, both excludes thoroughgoing iconoclasm and provides fresh resources for the working out of appropriate and inappropriate use of 'sacraments'; for theologically correct and incorrect artistic and sporting endeavours, for sexuality, intellectual and every other form of human creativity.

On the one hand, there is the fact that humanity is created to image God's own creativity, to embody the divine presence that is the source of all life, order and beauty. The image that is reconstituted in Israel understood very well how far this was a necessity for the healthy life of God's people. When Haggai tells the people that their ecological and economic crisis will only be averted by a full restoration of the temple and its worship (Hag. 1), it is the kind of iconographically rich and sacramentally centred world prescribed by the priestly material in the Pentateuch that is in mind. On the other hand, the Israelite critique of 'pagan' cultic practices can, equally, be turned against the religiosity of those who claim to stand within the biblical tradition. 'Liturgical' or 'sacramental' acts are merely 'magical' if they are means by which those who invest their faith in them avoid their responsibility to be, themselves, the Great Sacrament. Idolatry has to do, fundamentally, with a narcissistic avoidance of responsibility for bearing the divine image, for the good of the other. If Israelites make their sacrifices merely a matter of routine, whilst not at the same time practising the justice of their creator and saviour, if Christians 'celebrate' Jesus' death though they refuse to participate in its ethic and the continuing communication of its salvific power (as that is described, for example, by Paul in 2 Cor. 4.7–12 and Col. 1.24), then both abnegate their divine vocation in the same way as the idolaters among Israel's neighbours did. To this extent, Protestant criticisms of an absolute sacramental *ex opere operato* remain perceptive. However, by the same token, so much Protestant piety imagines a Christ, and his atoning work, that excuses his faithful from the hard work of the divine life. Whether or not this is the Jesus Christ of history and of New Testament faith – and we think it severely distorts the intention of the former and the reality of the latter – it is hard not to see in it yet another manifestation of the idolatrous refusal to bear the image, all the more insidious for its cloak of 'scriptural' and 'orthodox' respectability.

Notes

1 Neither *The Interpreter's Dictionary of the Bible* (G. A. Buttrick (ed.), Nashville, Tennessee: Abingdon, 1962) nor the *Anchor Bible Dictionary* (D. N. Freedman (ed.), New York: Doubleday, 1992), has entries for 'Sacraments', 'Sacramental'.

2 A now classic expression of a resurgence of interest in the comparative method and the correlation between myth and ritual is Jon D. Levenson, *Creation and the Persistence of Evil: The Jewish Drama of Divine Omnipotence* (San Francisco: HarperCollins, 1988), in which Levenson appeals for a rediscovery of the role of theurgy in Israel's religious life.

3 Jacob Milgrom and his pupils have contributed greatly to this sea change in scholarship. In what follows, I am particularly indebted to the groundbreaking work of Margaret Barker.

4 I have discussed this more fully elsewhere: 'The Worship of Divine Humanity and the Worship of Jesus', in C. C. Newman, J. R. Davila and G. Lewis (eds), *The Jewish Roots of Christological Monotheism: Papers from the St. Andrews Conference on the Historical Origins of the Worship of Jesus* (Leiden: Brill, 1999), pp. 112–28. Besides the literature cited there, see I. Provan, 'To Highlight all our idols: Worshipping God in Nietzsche's World', *Ex Auditu* 15 (1999), pp. 19–38 (esp. 25–26) and U. Mauser, 'God in Human Form', *Ex Auditu* 16 (2000), pp. 81–100.

5 See G. A. Jónsson, *The Image of God: Genesis 1.26–28 in a Century of Old Testament Research* (Stockholm: Almqvist & Wiksell, 1988), pp. 126–144.

6 See esp. M. Weinfeld, 'Sabbath, Temple and the Enthronement of the Lord: The Problem of the *Sitz-im-Leben* of Gen. 1:1–2:3', in A. Caquot and M. Delcor (eds), *Mélanges bibliques et orientaux en l'honneur de M. Henri Cazelles* (Neukirchen-Vluyn: Neukirchener Verlag, 1981), pp. 501–11.

7 M. Gruber, 'God, Image of', in J. Neusner (ed.), *The Encyclopaedia of Judaism: Supplement* (Leiden: Brill, 2003), pp. 1757–62 (esp. 1760–61).

8 H. Niehr, 'In Search of YHWH's Cult Statue in the First Temple', in K. van der Toorn (ed.), *The Image and the Book: Iconic Cults, Aniconism, and the Rise of Book Religion in Israel and the Ancient Near East* (Leuven: Peeters, 1997), pp. 73–96 (93–94).

9 S. D. McBride, 'Divine Protocol: Genesis 1:1–2:3 as Prologue to the Pentateuch', in W. P. Brown and S. D. McBride (eds), *God Who Creates. Essays in Honor of W. Sibley Towner* (Grand Rapids, MI: Eerdmans, 2003), pp. 3–41 (16–17).

10 McBride's 'blurring' of the otherwise sharp creator-creation distinction is infelicitous, but that, in some sense, the creator becomes the creature in humanity is surely an ineluctable conclusion of this new understanding of Gen. 1.26–27.

11 M. Barker, *The Great High Priest: The Temple Roots of Christian Liturgy* (London: T.&T. Clark, 2003), pp. 80, 152–54, 207, 227.

12 On the golden garments of the gods tradition, see A. L. Oppenheim, 'The Golden Garments of the Gods', *ANES* 4 (1949), pp. 172–193.

13 For the fuller text (in translation) and a discussion of its historical context see C. Walker, and M. B. Dick, *The Induction of the Cult Image in Ancient Mesopotamia: The Mesopotamian Mîs Pî Ritual* (Helsinki: The Neo-Assyrian Text Corpus Project, 2001), pp. 25–6.

14 For this Mesopotamian account of idol manufacture, compare also Jer. 10.1–16.

15 P. J. Kearney, 'Creation and Liturgy: The P Redaction of Exodus 25–40', *ZAW* 89 (1977), pp. 375–87 (375).

16 M. Barker, *The Great High Priest*, pp. 48, 61, 88.

17 Discussed in C. H. T. Fletcher-Louis, 'The High Priest as Divine Mediator in the Hebrew Bible: Dan. 7.13 as a Test Case', *Society of Biblical Literature Seminar Papers* (1997), pp. 161–93 (190–91).

18 M. Barker, 'The High Priest and the Worship of Jesus', in C. C. Newman, J. R. Davila and G. S. Lewis (eds), *The Jewish Roots of Christological Monotheism* (see note 4 above), pp. 93–111 (101–2); Fletcher-Louis, *All the Glory of Adam: Liturgical Anthropology in the Dead Sea Scrolls* (Studies on the Texts of the Desert of Judah, 42, Leiden: Brill, 2001), pp. 81–3. For a further exploration of the high priest's identification with the divine warrior see M. Barker, *The Revelation of Jesus Christ* (Edinburgh: T.&T. Clark, 2000), pp. 50–6.

19 See, further, Fletcher-Louis, *All the Glory of Adam*, pp. 395–475.

20 The evidence for this is discussed in J. Milgrom, *Numbers* (Philadelphia: Jewish Publication Society, 1990), pp. 413–14.

6

Sacraments as the Mystery of Union: elements in an Orthodox sacramental theology

Peter C. Bouteneff

In what follows I seek to discuss sacraments under the rubric of union between God and creation, between heaven and earth, since I believe this to be the most important thing to be said today about sacraments and sacramentality. Before that discussion, however, a note is in order as to why my title is confessionally specific. I am explicit in naming Orthodoxy, partly because I was invited to provide an Orthodox view and partly because of my reading of the contemporary ecumenical movement. Multilateral ecumenism has too hastily left the 'comparative method' and moved to the 'convergence method'. After several decades in the early twentieth century, when the Churches explained to each other what they believed and what they taught, it came to be felt that we knew all we needed to know about each other, and that it was time now only to say things together, to say them in common. The timing of the leap towards consensus method was appropriate for some, but not for the majority of the dialogue partners. Indeed, this move, together with the subsequent reluctance to check back periodically with confessional methodology (under the apprehension that to do so would constitute a step backwards), has been one of the main underlying causes of the estrangement from multilateral institutional ecumenism that is today being experienced broadly among the Churches. With few exceptions – the most notable being the 1982 Faith and Order text on *Baptism, Eucharist, and Ministry* (a sacramental theme, we note) – multilateral ecumenical texts and processes have left behind all but a few enthusiasts. This is certainly the case for my own Orthodox constituency. The fact is that we are all still getting to know each other as Churches, and to some degree every generation needs to start the process anew. This means that as much profit, interest and edification is gained from the exchange of ideas based on common lines of inquiry, there is also ecumenical value in speaking from our confessional identities, to the extent that these still exist. Having established that, what makes mine an 'Orthodox' synthesis? Almost none of the materials I draw on as evidence are the exclusive property of Orthodox; indeed much of what follows is simply church history. Bishop Geoffrey Rowell's contribution to this volume is a particularly clear example of the kinds of convergences in approaches one can happily find across ecclesiastical lines: Orthodoxy has no monopoly on orthodoxy. Nonetheless, if the methodology and the synthesis bear a certain Orthodox character, it is due not only to the special reliance on patristic texts and their enduring authority, but to the particular liturgical texts and practices that are the living context of the sacraments. These texts and rites, universally in use to the present day in Orthodox churches, lead to some inevitable conclusions within my confessional tradition. It is my hope that under any banner, under any church affiliation, my remarks might be of some use and some interest.

Mystery and sacrament

It is not insignificant that the word *sacramentum*, which has its own history in the Latin-speaking world (originally referring to initiation into the military), is rendered in the Christian East by the word *mysterion*. In Greek, in Syriac and in Slavic languages the words for 'sacrament' and 'mystery' continue to be the same.

To speak of a 'sacramental mystery' would be a redundancy, like saying 'holy saint'. Although we sometimes refer to sacraments (in particular the Eucharist) as 'the Holy Mysteries', those of us who speak Western languages need still to remind ourselves – in ways that Greek, Syriac and Russian speakers do not – of the interpenetration of the concepts of 'mystery' and of 'sacrament'. The Greek word *mysterion* (as well as the Russian *taina*, or the Syriac *raza/rozo*) accommodates both a wider sense of mystery (as something either hidden or something awesome) and a narrower sense of a rite, an action, which invokes the divine. Yet the interpenetration of the two senses goes beyond merely saying that the rites which we call 'sacraments' are in fact awesome, and often hidden, or exclusive in some way to the community of faith. The two senses find expression within the one word, bound together also by one overarching concept, namely that of *union*. Not 'unity', as in the static idea of oneness, but *union,* as in the dynamic action, the bringing together into unity of things that are divided.

Mystery as Union

From the intertestamental period onward, mysteries, especially in their ritual sense, have to do with the union between the human and the divine. That this is so in the pagan world as well is evident from what sparse information we can glean about the so-called 'mystery religions' which flourished especially from the first century BC through the fourth century AD. It is also clear that later Neo-Platonism, as we find it in Iamblichus and still later in Proclus, drew on mystery religions with their own theurgic rituals. Theurgy, a word with second-century origins, refers to rituals which tap into divine power, thus bringing down the gods – effectively uniting the divine and the earthly. In Christian usage, the ritual dimension of the word *mysterion* is evident – it refers to sacraments as a whole, as well as to the particular sacraments of Baptism and the Eucharist (again, uniting the divine and the earthly) – from at least the early fourth century.[1] Yet before *mysterion* comes to be used in the ritual sense, there are already multiple usages, as we can already see in Scripture. There, *mysterion* describes 'secrets' (Matt. 13.11 and parallels), things hidden (1 Cor. 2.7; Eph. 3.9; Col. 1.26), and matters of awesome depth (Rom. 11.25; 1 Cor. 4.1; 13.2; 15.51), often referring to the 'mystery' of God's awesome plan or his will for his creation. The various scriptural definitions are not mutually exclusive – it is more a matter of emphasis, in some places on hidden-ness or secrecy, in other places on awe and profundity. Mysteries, referring for example to some of Christ's own preaching, are 'hidden' in the sense that they are intended in the first instance for the community of faith. Christ says to his disciples at the telling of the parable of the sower, '*To you* it has been given to know the secrets (*mysteria*) of the kingdom of heaven . . .' (Matt. 13.11). The *mysteria* are, in this sense, hidden, shown to those set apart, called out. Yet as *mysteria* they are also matters for our awe, and ultimately unfathomable to human thought, ineffable. It is of significance that in at least two of the scriptural passages where *mysterion* takes on the sense of profundity and awe, the context is the theme of union. Both passages are from the letter to the Ephesians:

> For [the Father] has made known to us in all wisdom and insight the mystery of his will, according to his purpose which he set forth in Christ as a plan for the fullness of time, to unite all things in him, things in heaven and things on earth (*ta epi tois ouranois kai ta epi tês gês*). (Eph. 1.9f.)

> 'For this reason a man shall leave his father and mother and be joined to his wife, and the two shall become one flesh.' This *mysterion* is a profound one, and I am saying that it refers to Christ and the Church. (Eph. 5.31f.)

In the first passage, mystery is associated therefore with the unity of all things, in heaven and on earth, in Christ. In the second passage mystery is associated with the union between two distinct human persons, joined as one in the sacrament of love – a union made all the more profound by its explicit correlation to that between Christ and the Church. This latter passage is of interest in that Paul conflates the two so completely that it is difficult even to know precisely what he is referring to: the union of a man and a woman, or that between Christ and the Church. Throughout the passage, in virtually every verse (vv. 22–32), they seem each to illustrate the other and be illustrated by the other.[2]

There are several points to be gleaned from these two examples from the letter to the Ephesians. One is that, among the various usages of *mysterion*, we find that already within Scripture the ground is being laid for an understanding which has to do with the union of the uncreated with the created. That, as I shall continue to suggest, will be the chief rubric under which sacraments are considered, and from which they draw their significance for us and for our salvation. Another lesson from the second passage from Ephesians is that if sacrament/mystery, both in the broader and in the ritual sense, refers to the union between the uncreated and the created, marriage can properly be seen as a sacrament, a mystery. It is a sacrament, a '*mega mysterion*' for reasons made so clear by Paul: the union of two human persons as 'one flesh' does not end with these two alone. Marriage is evidently an icon of the union between Christ and the Church, between the divine and the human. Or rather marriage and the divine–human union image each other. This leads to a third point, which is supported strongly in the patristic writings as well as in the liturgy of the Church: union *with* Christ entails union *in* Christ. The old analogy of the wheel and its spokes is useful: as things travel along different spokes of a wheel towards its centre, their trajectory leads them closer not only to the centre but to each other. So sacramental unity is not only unity with God in Christ, it is unity with each other, unity with all that exists, in Christ.

Mysticism

Together with 'mystery' it is also worth considering here the words 'mystical' and 'mysticism'. In our day these are loaded with notions of hidden (or sometimes hazy) spirituality, associated with things too lofty to be considered, or even with the occult.

Going a bit farther back, mysticism has been understood in recent centuries as something *opposed* to theology, since theology has to do with expression and definition, and mysticism has to do with the unspeakable. Vladimir Lossky's *Mystical Theology of the Eastern Church* sets out to shatter such distinctions, saying that *all* theology is mystical. Indeed, Lossky calls mysticism 'the crown of theology', 'theology *par excellence'*.[3] This is so, precisely because mysticism is ultimately defined by its end: deification (*theosis*) – the *union of the divine and the human* within the human person. Lossky's linking of mystical theology with the goal of union is not novel. The very term 'mystical theology' was coined by the sixth-century author known as Dionysius the Areopagite (who also has something to say about sacraments). His shortest treatise, *Mystical Theology*, is an exhortation to his reader to 'strive upward as much as you can toward *union with him who is beyond all being and knowledge'*.[4] Even as it has to do with things hidden, things profound, things beyond speaking and beyond knowing, mysticism, like mystery, is ultimately about union.

Sacrament as Union

Having looked in this way at mystery, and associating it thoroughly with the activity of union, we can look again at sacraments (as rites) in the same terms. Sacraments, and let us take the Eucharist as the classic example, are all about the intersection of the human and the divine. Sacraments are about uniting the earthly with the heavenly, the time-bound with the eternal, the spatial with the non-circumscribable. Sacraments are often associated with *symbols*, but we need to examine that word as well. For if by symbol we mean a sign which bears no other presence than itself, which does nothing but illustrate something or point somewhere, we are doing justice neither to the ancients' understanding of symbol nor the reality of sacrament. The 'symbolic' character of sacraments is not merely illustrative or somehow evocative of a sense of the reality they are symbolizing. Alexander Schmemann says that '. . . the symbol does not so much "resemble" the reality that it symbolizes as it *participates*

in it, and therefore is capable of communicating it in reality'.[5]
Symbol, derived from the Greek roots *sym-* and *vallo*, literally to
'throw together' or to hold in unity, bespeaks the epiphanic presence of one reality within the other. The sacraments, as rites of
the Church, involve earthly elements like bread, wine, water,
and oil, elements which become 'symbolic' vehicles of divine
presence and action. Neither does the symbolic character of
these elements undermine the reality of the divine manifest in
them, nor does the divine in them make them cease to be what
they were – bread, wine, water, oil. One can talk in effect of 'two
natures in union without confusion'.

Christ as sacrament

That kind of language of course leads us inevitably to Christ
himself. Christ, the perfect union of the divine and the human,
is in his own person the ultimate sacrament, the paradigm of all
sacraments. All human attempts to bring themselves into communion with God, and all of God's searches for the fallen human
person, are fulfilled in the mystical union (if it is not redundant
to put it that way) of God and human in the single, unique
person of Jesus Christ. Even Scripture, at two points (Col. 2.2;
1 Tim. 3.16), appears to refer to Christ as '*the* mystery of God',[6]
or we might say the sacrament of God. Considering the two
natures, or the two consubstantialities – for Jesus is consubstantial both with humanity and with divinity – the Chalcedonian
adverbs are significant: two natures, says the *horos*, 'without confusion, without change, without division, and without separation'.[7] Once again, neither does the human stop being human,
nor does the divine stop being divine, but rather, as Orthodox
hymnography often puts it, 'the natures are made new'.[8] Thus,
the sacrament, the mystery that is the person of Jesus Christ, is
the paradigm of the union of divine and human in all sacramentality. In Christ, as with 'the sacraments', the initiative is on the
part of the divine, yet it requires human cooperation (*synergeia*)
and obedience (Heb. 5.8). In Christ, as with 'the sacraments', we
see that, because the divine chooses a self-emptying (*kenosis*), the

human is divinized, that is, brought to the state for which it was created, the state of free and loving communion with the divine, partaking of the divine nature (2 Pet. 1.4). In Christ, as with 'the sacraments', we also witness a union in which distinction and particularity is retained. For distinction is neither separation nor division, and the union preserves the integrity of the things united. This is vital: a distinction need not be obliterated when two things are brought into union – hence the concept of unity in diversity, and diversity in unity. The Christian concept of the unity to be striven for – namely a holding together of diversity, a union or holding-together of *logoi* in the *Logos*, as Maximus the Confessor would put it – is altogether different from the classical Greek philosophical ideal of unity, wherein the diversity of things *in and of itself* placed them lower on the scale of being, testifying to their ontological distance from The One. Indeed, the Christian ideal of unity – as unity in diversity – is exemplified in Christ, as well as in that other great *mysterion*, the diversity in unity that is the Holy Trinity.

The reckoning of sacraments

In discussing the broader and narrower interpretations of the words *sacramentum* and *mysterion*, we have noticed that at least as early as the fourth century *mysterion* denotes Baptism and the Eucharist, even as it refers to much broader and wider realities. What, in the ritual sense, can properly be called 'a sacrament'? When the question comes to how many sacraments there are, or to lists of the sacraments, there is no fixed teaching in the Orthodox Church. For centuries, 'the sacraments' were Baptism and the Eucharist. Dionysius the Pseudo-Areopagite (sixth century) adds ordination, monastic tonsure and Christian burial, but the sacraments are not 'counted' as such, or given a number, until the eighth or ninth centuries. Theodore Studite lists six: Baptism, Eucharist, Chrismation, Ordination, monastic tonsure and burial. Later lists (thirteenth to seventeenth centuries) tend to enumerate seven, for several reasons. Originally the listing of seven sacraments in the Christian East is owed to the influence of the Christian West: the emperor Michael Palaeologus, largely for political reasons, bowed to Roman conventions in his *Profession of Faith* and made it a point to count seven sacraments, but of course the number seven is full of significance, signifying completeness, and being the number of the 'gifts of the Spirit' described in Isaiah 11.2–4. Yet even the lists of seven vary as to their contents. Gregory Palamas in the fourteenth century goes back to listing only Baptism and Eucharist; his contemporary Nicholas Cabasilas adds also the consecration of a church. This testifies to a healthy fluidity in the reckoning of sacraments. Sacramentality, as referring to the profound union exemplified by Christ himself, does not lend itself to being set in stone in fixed lists of rites. On the one hand, this suggests a broader view of sacramentality, extending to the universal human vocation of raising all of creation up to God. Yet there remain particular rites that are singled out for that function, which can be called 'sacraments' in a way that other events and actions, no matter how unitive and God-pleasing, are not. As to what it is that unites them under that name, the following would constitute the beginnings of a response.[9]

- In the first instance, sacraments all refer to Christ. His institution of these rites, as testified in the last supper and in the great commission, is of course of significance. But sacraments bring us to Christ that we might partake of the same union of divine and human natures that he embodies in his own person. A beautiful passage in St Irenaeus of Lyons, *Against the Heresies,* sets out the way in which, if one believes in the union of God and human in Christ, the rites of Baptism and Eucharist naturally follow, as they express fully that union which brings the New Adam.[10] So the *mysteria*, Baptism and Eucharist, reveal the one *mysterion*.
- As anything that involves and refers to Christ, the sacraments bear a special relationship to the Holy Spirit, the Spirit which is called not only comforter or Paraclete, not only the Spirit of Truth and giver of life, but also the Spirit by whom God calls all to unity.[11]
- The sacraments are ecclesial rites. Ecclesial here means not only

communal, but also pertaining to the Church. Even as sacraments have universal significance and pertain to the union of all that is, they are performed in the Church, and for its members. As we saw above, the 'mysteries' retain the broader meaning of 'things hidden', in the sense that they are intended in the first instance for the community of faith, and through that community to the whole of creation.

- All the sacraments, not just Baptism and the Eucharist, communicate the one *mysterion,* Christ. They communicate Christ by manifesting him and enabling us to partake of him, and they do so particularly through their relationship to the Eucharist, which of course is pre-eminent among the rites we call sacraments. It is in their participation in the Eucharist that persons are seen as fully members of the Church (the Body of Christ) and of one another, and it is in their relation to the Eucharist that rites are understood as sacraments.

As just some examples of the above relationship, one may point to the following:

- Baptism is the rite of entry into the life in Christ, entry also into sacramental life, in the sacramental community of the Church. With Chrismation, the completion of the rite of entry, Baptism is fulfilled in the Eucharist, and the life in Christ, the membership in the body of Christ, is sustained in the Eucharist.
- Ordinations are always performed during the eucharistic liturgy, and for the eucharistic liturgy. (At the service of ordination, the ordinand is given the tools he will need to fulfil his function within the Eucharist.) The authority of the ordination is also grounded in the eucharistic community.
- Penance originates as a restoration to the eucharistic communion of the Church; anointing also has to do with reconciliation with Christ and restoration to communion.

So there are certain features which can be said to describe the rites which come to be reckoned as 'sacraments', and they have to do with union in general, and specifically with Christ, with the Church and with the Eucharist.

Sacraments and Union in the Eucharist

The Eucharist has just been shown to be the sacramental rite *par excellence*, the foundation of sacraments. The Eucharist, which of course is often referred to as 'Holy Communion', is illustrative in a particular way of how the sacraments in the Church are all about union. Not only does the Eucharist 'throw together' the divine and the earthly in the elements of bread and wine, which come also to be for us the body and blood of Christ, but in our common union in these gifts and in our partaking of them, we participate in the union of everything that exists. It is the spokes-in-the-wheel image which again springs to mind: the closer one is to the centre, the closer one is to the neighbour. The eucharistic liturgies in use to this day in the Orthodox Church, those of St John Chrysostom and St Basil the Great, testify explicitly to the effecting of union with Christ and with everyone and everything. They speak in the first instance of a union among those assembled at the liturgy: the credal confession of faith begins with the exclamation, 'Let us love one another, that with one mind we may confess the Father, Son, and Holy Spirit, the Trinity consubstantial and undivided'. The Liturgy of St Basil is particularly evocative of the theme of union – of the assembly with each other, and with the world, and of all with God – in the lengthy canon of prayers said before and after the *epiclesis* (an *epiclesis* which invokes the Holy Spirit 'upon *us*, and upon these gifts here set forth'). The theme is introduced perfectly in a short prayer recited immediately after the *epiclesis*, which begins thus: 'And unite all of us to one another who become partakers of the one bread and cup in the communion of the Holy Spirit'. The ensuing series of prayers seeks effectively to unite not only those present at the particular eucharistic celebration, but also all people; they enumerate all kinds of situations, particularly those of need. These prayers call on God to 'remember' people and situations, a remembrance that brings them also into communion with us. Moreover, it is a remembrance which calls us into an awareness of the social dimension of the Eucharist, the responsibility that we have for each other, and particularly for the poor

101

and the needy. Below is a partial enumeration of those whom we call upon God to remember in the eucharistic canon of the Liturgy of St Basil:

- All who have died before us in the hope of resurrection to eternal life (naming also specific persons);
- The Church universal, as well as the local church;
- Those who remember the poor;
- Those in the deserts, mountains, caverns, and pits of the earth;
- Those who live in chastity and godliness, in austerity and holiness of life;
- This country and those who dwell in it;
- The civil authorities ('grant them a lasting peace, speak good things into their hearts . . . so that we, in their tranquillity, may lead a calm and peaceful life in all godliness and sanctity');
- Those who serve in the armed forces;
- Those present, and also those absent for good reason;
- Those held captive by unclean spirits;
- Travellers, the sick, widows, orphans;
- Those in courts, in mines, in exile, in harsh labour;
- Those in any kind of affliction, necessity or distress;
- Those who love us, and those who hate us.

Having brought these into communion through God's remembrance, we also pray that God will act in specific ways towards everyone, asking that God 'preserve their marriages in peace and harmony, raise the infants, guide the young, support the aged, encourage the faint-hearted'. At this point, significantly, we ask that God 'reunite the separated', a request for union in a very general sense. The prayer goes on to ask God to bring apostates back into the Church, and later still asks God to 'prevent schisms among the churches', but that is not all that we are praying for in asking God to bring back into unity any who have been separated. This concern testifies to the Christian conviction that redeemed existence has a lot to do with union. (One of the names of the devil is of course *ho diavolos* – the divider, the one who 'throws apart'.) Indeed, the enlightenment moments within many religious traditions revolve around the realization of the profound unity underlying all things. The prayers become now very general in again asking God to remember *everyone*: 'those who love us, those who hate us . . . remember all your people, O Lord our God. Pour out your rich mercy upon all of them . . . Remember yourself, O God, all those whom we have not remembered, through ignorance, forgetfulness, or the multitude of names . . .'

Aside from the texts of the liturgy, some of the Church's most important and influential writers and preachers – most notably the liturgical authors themselves, Basil the Great and John Chrysostom – also had a profound sense that the sacrament of the eucharistic liturgy entails a 'liturgy after the liturgy'. St John likes to allude to two altars, that in the church, and that in the public space. The first, we rightly revere. The second, we ignore, and it is the poor, the suffering, those in need, the homeless, all who are in distress.[12]

> Do you wish to honour the Body of the Saviour? Do not despise it when it is naked. Do not honour it in church with silk vestments while outside it is naked and numb with cold. He who said, 'This is my body', and made it so by his word, is the same who said, 'You saw me hungry and you gave me no food. As you did it not to the least of these, you did it not to me'. Honour him then by sharing your property with the poor, for what God needs is not golden chalices but golden souls.[13]

The eucharistic liturgy, in practice and in contemplation, in celebration and in thought and action, is thus quite explicit in its testimony to the belief that not only are we united with Christ as we partake of him, but in partaking of him we are brought into union with each other in the community of faith, and with all that exists.

The 'stuff' of sacraments

During the rite of blessing anything, whether bread, or water, or wine, or oil, we say that we are uniting the earthly and the heavenly, bringing the earthly element to the state for which it was created. Water becomes what it is supposed to be, life-giving and refreshing. Bread becomes what it is supposed to be, nourishing not only the body but the soul. Oil becomes the oil of gladness,

103

the oil of a priestly anointing, for all are anointed as priests – to embark on the priestly vocation of lifting up the whole of creation to God. Ordinary, basic human actions are brought into the context of salvation through the rites of the sacrament. In the Eucharist, an ordinary meal becomes a means of communion with God; washing becomes Baptism; the human contract of cohabitation becomes Christian marriage; anointing becomes something that effects healing, reconciliation, and forgiveness.[14] In all of this we begin to see, among other things, a theology of matter, one which follows on the powerful conviction of Orthodox theology that creation, though fallen, is *good*. In certain moods, in certain manners of speaking, the early Christian writers could lapse into Platonic language which lamented the imprisonment of the immaterial soul in the material body. Yet as a whole, and when it actually came down to elaborating a doctrine of creation, they were profoundly holistic, defending against the pagans the sanctified character of matter, the organic unity and interdependence of the human body and soul, the joy of Christ's incarnation into space, time and matter, and the eternal resurrection, which is bodily. When, therefore, it comes to matter, the Orthodox Church has always stressed in its own way the 'stuff' of the world, even as it offers that stuff to God, so that God may make it what it is truly supposed to be. I wonder if this is one of the reasons we stress leavened bread for the Eucharist, why we continue to insist on Baptism by full immersion into water, why we kiss our icons. We like this 'stuff' and plunge ourselves into it, chew it, kiss it. Speaking of icons, of course, the defence of matter comes to a particular test when it comes to the iconoclastic controversy. At the seventh ecumenical council, it was affirmed that 'the honour given to the [material] icon is conveyed to the prototype'. Likewise, St John Damascene said, in a well-known passage,

> In former times, God, who is without form or body, could never be depicted. But now when God is seen in the flesh conversing with men, I make an image of the God whom I see. I do not worship matter; I worship the Creator of matter who became matter for my

sake, who willed to take His abode in matter; who worked out my salvation through matter. Never will I cease honouring the matter which wrought my salvation![15]

Conclusion

A sacramental theology has much to hold together, and yet much to give integrity and wholeness. Recalling the words 'mystery' and 'mystical' and their multiple dimensions, broader and narrower, seeing how these in turn play out in the words 'sacrament' and 'sacramental', again with broader and narrower meanings, we are continually reminded how in each instance there is ultimately a reference to the coming together of the uncreated and the created, to the meeting of the uncircumscribable with the material; to the timeless stepping into time. We are left with the question about the extent to which we can properly apply the word and the concept of sacramentality outside the ecclesiastical rites which we call sacraments. In so far as there is indeed a broader meaning to the word sacrament/*mysterion*, one which precedes the ritual, narrower meaning, of course we can use the word sacrament more broadly. Anything that pertains to union with the other and with the sacred could in some sense be called sacramental. One's experience of music, art, food, sex, can be transcendent, epiphanic, and in this way termed 'sacramental' in a qualitative way. Indeed, we do well to open out our sense of the sacramental, and to see in any and every moment of life the potential for a greater union with the other, with creation, and with God himself. In a sense, all of life is sacrament, only awaiting our realization of it. The broader definition of sacrament may have preceded the narrower, but something has changed in the world: Christ has come, the Church has come. We now have the unique and miraculous gift of the sacramental rites, founded in the sacrament that is Christ himself, the rites performed uniquely in and through the Church, for the world. And now it is these rites which have become definitive, archetypal of sacramentality. All of life *is* sacrament just as all the world is created good, created for holiness. Yet just as there are places, people, things, that are 'set apart' as holy, through which the world recalls its holiness, so there are the particular rites within the 'set-apart' holy community of the Church, through which the world recalls its true sacramentality. If we relativize the Church's sacraments, seeing them as but expressions (alongside others) of the union of heaven and earth, we deprive sacramentality of any but the haziest meaning. 'Sacramentality' is in danger of taking its place alongside other neutered words, like 'spirituality'. Sacraments are the ground of the sacramental, and this is the joy of all creation.

Notes

1 Cf. Eusebius, *Demonstratio evangelica* 9.6 (*PG* 22, 673C); Athanasius, *Contra Arianos* 2.42 (*PG* 26, 236C); Basil of Caesarea, *De Spiritu Sancto* 66 (*PG* 32, 188B).

2 We find the same approach suggested when Christ calls himself 'the bridegroom' in Matt. 9.15 and parallels.

3 V. Lossky, *The Mystical Theology of the Eastern Church* (Crestwood, NY: SVS, 1976), p. 9. (Originally published in 1944 in French, as *Essai sur la théologie mystique de l'Eglise d'Orient.*)

4 Emphasis added.

5 Alexander Schmemann, *The Eucharist* (Crestwood, NY: SVS, 1988), p. 38.

6 In each case, the Greek original is not entirely clear as to whether *mysterion* refers to Christ himself. In Col. 2.2, (. . . eis epignôsin tou mystēriou tou theou kai partos kai tou christou) St Paul is either speaking of 'the mystery of God, namely Christ', or 'the mystery of God – of the Father – and of Christ'. A similar ambiguity, reflected in the different translations and relying on variances in Greek manuscripts, exists in 1 Tim. 3.16 (. . . mega estin to tēs eusebias *mystērion* [theos] ephanerôthē en sarki . . .).

7 Modern bilateral agreements between 'Orthodox' (Chalcedonian) and 'Oriental Orthodox' (non-Chalcedonian) Churches indicate universal acceptance of the language of 'double consubstantiality'

as well as of the famous four adverbs of the Chalcedonian definition.

8 For example, Ode 7, Canon on the Sunday of the Blind Man,
where we sing about the Incarnation: 'God made natures new by
his power . . .'

9 I am grateful to my colleague Paul Meyendorff for an outline of
the list that follows.

10 Irenaeus, *Adversus Haereses*, V. iii. 1: 'Vain also are the Ebionites,
who do not receive by faith into their soul the union of God and
man, but who remain in the old leaven of the natural birth. For
they choose not to understand that the Holy Spirit came upon
Mary, and the power of the Most High overshadowed her: and
therefore what was generated is a holy thing. The Son of the Most
High God the Father of all, who effected the incarnation of this
being, thus showed forth a new kind of generation [Baptism (PB)];
so that by the former generation we inherited death, so by this new
generation we might inherit life. Therefore these people reject the
commixture of the heavenly wine [Eucharist (PB)], and wish it to
be water of the world only, not receiving God so as to have union
with Him. They remain rather in that Adam who had been conquered and was expelled from Paradise . . .'

11 Kontakion for the Feast of Pentecost, referring to Babel and
Pentecost respectively: 'When the Most High came down and confused the tongues he divided the nations. But when he distributed
the tongues of fire he called all to unity . . .'

12 See, for example, John Chrysostom, *Hom. in Heb.*, XI.

13 John Chrysostom, *Hom. in Matt.*, 50, iii, iv.

14 With gratitude again to Paul Meyendorff.

15 John of Damascus, *First Apology Against Those Who Attack Divine
Images*, 16.

7

Feminist theology and sacramental theology: old and new challenges

Susan A. Ross

To address the rather broad topic of 'feminist theology and sacramental theology' in a brief article is, of course, an impossible task. Feminist theology represents a very diverse collection of theological perspectives that cut across not only the various Christian denominational traditions but also differing and sometimes even opposing theoretical positions within feminism itself. Sacramental theology, too, is a diverse field of study. Does one mean sacramentality in the broad sense? Does one mean the particular sacraments? Or are we speaking of ecumenical perspectives on the sacraments? Even in the field of sacramental theology we do not always agree on such issues as presence, the role of philosophy, not to mention the issues that feminist theologians raise. So with these caveats in mind, I propose to outline three sets of questions that are of concern to me: an American feminist theologian who teaches in a Catholic university in the United States of America and is also a 'practising' Catholic. I like to think that when I am practising my Catholicism, I am trying, as I do when I practise the piano, to improve my understanding, skills and appreciation of the tradition. Yet I am also bringing my own sets of issues and questions to that same tradition and I therefore seek then not just to perform it as written but to improvise upon it as well. Thinking of the sacramental tradition as a set of musical scores is certainly not new or original to me, but I find the metaphor helpful in this particular context. Christian feminist theologians seek to do at least three things: to raise critical questions about the ways that the Christian tradition has both understood and misunderstood women; to bring to the fore our concerns for the voices that have been marginalized or silenced, both in the past and in the present; and to undertake the task that we all share as theologians of presenting the tradition anew in ways that are faithful, truthful and compelling. When it comes to sacramental theology, feminist theologians have raised critical questions about ordained ministry and related assumptions about the role of gender in our thinking about human nature, Christ, and God.[1] We have questioned the rhetoric of equality and unity in our eucharistic practice on behalf not only of women but also of those who suffer from what Rosemary Radford Ruether calls 'eucharistic famine'.[2] We have improvised on the sacramental tradition, developing new liturgical practices that address the needs and concerns of women's distinct experiences.[3] We have explored the dynamics of sacramentality along the lines of postmodernity, and questioned the place of gender in these theories.[4] And we have also worked to link more closely the work of justice and our liturgical celebrations.[5] In this article, I would like to focus on three sets of related issues that are, in various ways, feminist variations on old themes, as well as being new ways of playing the score that may sound, to some, as if the traditional music is no longer the same. They are, first, some reflections on embodiment and postmodern thought on sacraments through a feminist lens; second, some reflections on ecclesiology and feminist sacramental practice; third, some thoughts on the relationships among women, the sacraments, beauty, and justice.

I will attempt to begin a conversation here between feminist theology and sacramental theology in relation to these three issues, suggesting that there are questions on the part of each for the other and that unless these questions are seriously engaged by both, little movement forward is likely. I take my cue from Kathryn Tanner, who suggests that feminist theologians seriously engage with the tradition, not just attempt to break away and create new traditions.[6] Her point is that without doing so, feminist theology is unlikely to have much of an impact beyond its own circle and thus will ultimately fail to effect the transformation it so desires.

The body, women and postmodernity

Like nearly every field of study in theology, sacramental theology has been influenced by postmodern thought. Particularly in the works of Jean-Luc Marion, Louis-Marie Chauvet and David Power, sacramental theologians have sought to uncouple ontotheology and the sacraments by turning away from metaphysics and its tendency to totalize our thinking and to turn 'real presence' into an object there for our grasping.[7] In this fragmented world, our ability to know and grasp not only others but God as well has come under deep suspicion. Both Marion and Chauvet have sought to reinterpret the understanding of real presence, although they end up with different results. Yet for both, the emphasis is on the otherness of God and our human inability to grasp this otherness. Where, for Marion, the doctrine of transubstantiation most adequately preserves the divine otherness, for Chauvet the presence of Christ is found not in the sacrament's otherness but in the community where the Eucharist is celebrated. What emerges as key for postmodernity is the emphasis on the other, both the others we encounter in our daily lives and the Wholly Other who invites us into fullness of life. The emphasis on the Other is a significant move in theology.[8] But I would ask whether, from a feminist perspective, this turn to the Other adequately addresses the issues that women face in sacramental theology and worship. Here I have in mind the role of the body.

In my book on feminist theology and the sacraments, I questioned whether Chauvet's understanding of sacraments as the mediation of the presence of the absent God did justice to women's experiences. Given how Chauvet draws on the work of Lacan, I asked whether the desire to experience God in some unmediated fashion – the desire that Chauvet argues is at the root of human experience, language and the sacraments – is as characteristic of women as it is of men. My concern was that the Lacanian theory of language and development did not adequately take into account women's developmental experiences nor did it draw on some of the feminist critiques of Lacan that question the nature of the subject's relation to language, symbol and mediation.[9] I continue to have some questions about Lacan's theories and their relation to women's experiences, but in thinking through some of these issues again I would want to add now that I find Chauvet's theories more open to a feminist understanding of the significance of embodiment. Chauvet has been criticized for his failure to take his critique of ontotheology far enough.[10] That is, in his conviction that the real presence of Christ is found in the worshipping community, he runs the risk of limiting God again to the human, which is the problem with a metaphysical conception of presence. Nevertheless, I find in Chauvet's thinking a more hospitable openness to embodiment and materiality, ideas that are not only central to feminist thought but to sacrament and sacramentality as well. Towards the end of *Symbol and Sacrament*, Chauvet discusses the relation of the Son to the Father and says:

> Therefore, it is impossible to separate the divine *kenosis* from the one that must be carried out in ourselves: our corporality is charged with becoming the place for this *kenosis*. In our corporality, the most distant is also the closest; the most divine is the most human . . . Thus we are obliged to give to this God the body of humanity that God asks of us. Corporality is God's place . . . God, whose being is not 'to be' . . . reduced to nothing as God has been by humankind, finds God's 'sacrament' in those who have themselves been reduced to 'not-others'.[11]

It is by now a familiar truism to say that feminist theology attempts to reclaim the significance of the body. Yet the extent to which real bodies, bodies that bleed, are seen as the place of the divine, is another question altogether. In spring 2003, at a reception for Ida Raming, one of the women ordained on a boat in the Danube in the summer of 2002, I found myself in conversation with Carolyn Osiek, a New Testament scholar. We were talking about how one responds to the question of women's ordination in public lectures, and she told me that when asked why women could not be ordained, she would answer simply 'blood'. 'Blood', of course, is not the entire answer, but it refers to the constellation of issues surrounding women's embodiment: sexuality, materiality, and, in theological terms, their contrast with the divine, with the Word, with the conceptual dimension of human life, with the spirit. Blood, body, sexuality and materiality are also clues to what is understood to be explicitly Judaeo-Christian in some senses: that is, that Judaism and Christianity are not tied to nature, but to the Word; not to endless natural cycles, but to history; not to the female goddess of fertility but to the transcendent yet seminal Word. Yet Judaism and particularly Christianity are also inexorably tied to the material through the Incarnation.[12] The ambiguity of materiality is most evident in the Christian tradition's uneasiness with the linkage of women, sexuality, and the sacred.

While Chauvet has not carried through the relevance of these ideas to feminist questions in sacramental theology, my suggestion is that there is no reason why this should not be done. In particular, the feminist concern with the concrete conditions of women's lives and Chauvet's concern with corporality have the potential to push our thinking on real presence through and beyond arguments about women's fitness for ordination to a more adequate sense of real presence and the need for justice. This is not to say, however, that I would merely dismiss the question of women's ordination, particularly as it remains a contested issue in my own tradition. In the fall of 2003, the newspapers reported a new effort on the part of the Vatican to exclude girl altar servers and lay preachers who, it is claimed, 'usurp' the role of the priest.[13] The exclusion of women from the altar is not just a question of justice – although it is that – but it also remains a scandal in the true sense of the word: an obstacle to further conversation and development. For many feminist thinkers, the refusal to allow serious conversation on women's ordination is evidence of dangerous mystification: the appeal to ideas beyond human ken and serious investigation but known for sure by those in power. Moreover, the unease with women's physical presence in the sanctuary evidences a scandalous refusal to take incarnation seriously. But, as I have argued elsewhere, the issue of real presence has nothing to do with gender and everything to do with justice.[14] This is not to say that gender is irrelevant, but that a focus on gender alone can distort the real opportunities that could exist for challenging the people of God to be the real presence of Christ in their communities. It is in the scandal of particularity that the real presence is found. And while the concerns of Marion and others to preserve the otherness of God are in many ways an essential reminder and a caution to the tradition, my own concern, both as a feminist and a Catholic one, is that it is in the scandalous *particularity* of the Incarnation that its relevance to all human beings is found. In other words, it is not maleness, or Palestinian-ness, but human bodiliness that is so scandalously particular. And it is in God's refusal to be wholly absent and wholly other and rather to be historically, and thus partially and fragmentarily present to us in our embodiment. Chauvet's reflections on corporality and *kenosis* cut, I think, to the heart of the matter: it is in the most human of places, the body of a woman, that incarnation took place, and continues to take place, in the lives of women and men born of women. The neuralgic issue of ordination, then, is not the primary question here (although it remains a significant one), but rather our willingness to take seriously the radical idea of incarnation, specifically incarnation in the body of the other. Thus the issues of the linkage of the body to blood and nature and ideas of gender complementarity need to be understood in the primary light of the real presence. Feminist theology contributes to this conversation its rejection of literalized metaphor, particularly its criticism of romantic and idealized notions of femininity in relation to the divine. Yet what the tradition contributes here is its rich poetic tradition, one which sees reality as having a deeper meaning than what is immediately seen. Because of limitations of time and space, I can only hint here at the possibilities, but I would suggest, taking a cue from Teresa Berger, that taking feminist ritual seriously will provide a richer basis for an adequate understanding of our liturgical and sacramental traditions – becoming less Eucharist-centred, so to speak – and for feminist theology, grappling with the rich symbolism of the tradition, particularly its understanding of Mary and the saints as well as the resources from women's spirituality over the centuries.[15] Feminist theologians need to explore more fully the role of embodiment, and the mainstream tradition needs to draw more closely on its own rich metaphoric tradition in the richest possible ways.

Church

The second issue that I would like to explore was suggested to me recently, as I read Peter Steinfels' new book, *A People Adrift: The Crisis of the Roman Catholic Church in America*.[16] In this book Steinfels comments on what he sees as the fluidity of Catholic feminist theology and some of the problems this raises. In a chapter entitled 'Sex and the Female Church', Steinfels describes a Women-Church gathering in 1993, where, for many women, their relationship to the institutional Church was, if not ridiculed, certainly downplayed. One woman he quotes identified herself as being 'from – and I emphasize *from* – [. . .] the Roman Catholic Church'.[17] At least for Steinfels, the meeting took on what he calls a 'religious smørgåsbord' of ritual practice and raised some serious ecclesiological questions. Steinfels describes these as the 'two complications of feminism – its unreadiness or incapacity to address boundaries and its distance from many Catholic women'.[18] Steinfels identifies Catholic feminist theology as 'fluid, amorphous, and unfixed'.[19] He says, 'Much Catholic feminist thought is relatively uninterested in the whole question of differentiating what is compatible with Catholic Christianity from what is not, and at present is underequipped to do so'. He sees Catholic feminist theology as 'teetering on the edge of secession'.[20] These are serious charges, and while I think he ignores some very real and significant distinctions between Catholic and Protestant feminist thinkers, I think he is basically correct in noting that, for many of these women, it is at least somewhat premature to work on the question of what constitutes a more adequate Catholic position than another. One of Steinfels' real concerns is that this lack of boundaries distances Catholic feminist theology from 'the woman in the pew'. I have two observations in relation to this point. The first is in relation to the centrality of the Eucharist in the Catholic tradition. The second has to do with hierarchy and community. Steinfels appeals to the 'woman in the pew' for whom questions like, 'Can a male saviour save women?' and 'Must we use inclusive language?' are, he argues, somewhat remote. I take it from his remarks that, for him, the woman in the pew basically has no argument with the technicalities of theology and is more concerned with whether or not there is a good religious education programme in her parish and if Mass will let her out on time for her to get to her children's soccer game. Perhaps, but I think Steinfels might underestimate the 'woman in the pew'.

Religious communities of women have been grappling with the issue of the Eucharist for some time now. Their difficulties emerge from the fact that they must have someone from outside their community to come in order for them to have a valid Eucharist. Their eucharistic leadership cannot come from within their community, and although I have seen some very creative ways of dealing with this situation, it does not erase the point that while men's religious communities can have a true community Eucharist, women's religious communities cannot. To be quite blunt, 'Father' must come in, and it does not matter who 'Father' is, so long as he is 'Father'. I have written elsewhere about this situation and suggested some possible ways of facing this situation with creativity and honesty.[21] But I think that these communities of nuns are somewhat like the proverbial canary in the mineshaft. That is, as more and more religious and parish communities deal with the fact that their pastors may be responsible for more than one parish and may well find themselves stretched to the limits to meet the many needs that their communities have, communities will be forced to think more deeply about the role of Eucharist in their lives and its leadership. I have suggested elsewhere that there is a very real way in which the Eucharist has completely overtaken other devotions, and I think that the growth in the popularity of non-eucharistic devotions among young people is one symptom of the effect that this centring of all liturgical activity in the Eucharist has had.[22] This point also raises other questions about the quality of eucharistic worship, but I will not pursue those here. The issue, then, of the relationship of eucharistic presiding to the community is *not* simply a 'women's issue' or a question raised by 'radical nuns'. With all due respect to Steinfels, I think that he overlooks the wider implications of centring all liturgy in the Eucharist. While the Eucharist is, as Vatican II puts it, 'the fount and summit of the Church's liturgical life', it is not our only sacramental opportunity for worship. I mean this in both a practical and a theological sense. That is, practically speaking, many today are unable to participate in the Eucharist because there is no priest. However, the answer to this is not simply more priests, but a careful thinking and rethinking about the nature of our sacramental worship.

This leads to my second point about feminist and sacramental theology and community. Feminist theologians have raised serious questions about church polity and, in some cases, argue that any form of hierarchy is intrinsically evil. I am less inclined myself to take that route, having had some experience of the pluses and minuses of congregationalism. Nevertheless, feminist theologians do push the envelope of denominational membership and challenge traditional structures of organization. But they are not alone in doing this. In a recent article in *Theological Studies*, Peter Phan writes about the phenomenon of multiple religious belonging.[23] I found his treatment of the issue very interesting and helpful, but I was also interested in the fact that there was no mention of this phenomenon as it relates to feminist theology or disaffected women and their religious traditions. I would note that what is occurring with women's reluctance to hold to denominational boundaries is very much in line with what is happening in the larger public sphere, where a looser sense of religious membership is at work. While there is a genuine difference, in that many feminist women are, unlike those in Phan's observations, 'disaffected', the point of living with ambiguity and tensions and the need to be better educated is a very important issue. I would agree with Phan that these trends suggest a need for greater openness to the truths of other traditions, as well as a need to experience these more intensely. Nevertheless, Christian feminist theologians cannot simply dismiss the centrality of certain dimensions of Christian faith if they wish to remain so. I would suggest at this point that feminist theologians scrutinize carefully their own eucharistic theology as much as I would argue that the tradition that many feminists find so frustrating needs to undertake a similar scrutiny as to the aim of eucharistic celebration.

Theological aesthetics

The attention given to theological aesthetics over the last ten or fifteen years is, I think, no surprise, given the state of liturgy and theology today. Many of us can tell of countless instances of dreadful but sincere liturgy that has little sense of beauty or transcendence. While feminist theologians have, for the most part, paid little attention to the discussions in theological aesthetics for a number of good reasons, and while concerns for justice have for many feminists taken precedence over concerns for beauty, I think that there is room for challenge and discussion here as well. Let me briefly outline just two points. Those familiar with the work of Hans Urs von Balthasar are no doubt also familiar with the significance of nuptial metaphors in his work and the central place of Mary. For von Balthasar, as well as for Pope John Paul II, theological anthropology has a profoundly Marian form, as humanity models itself on the receptive, affirming, and obediential stance of Mary towards God. It is, in fact, impossible to understand von Balthasar's theological aesthetics without attention to gender and the place of Mary and the feminine.[24] Feminist theologians have not found in von Balthasar a congenial conversation partner for many good reasons, not least his understanding of the role of the 'feminine'. Indeed, feminist theology has largely been critical of approaches to theology that (over)emphasize the transcendent dimension of the divine, because of their tendency to relegate completely the 'feminine' to the side of the human part of the relationship. Notwithstanding the many inherent problems in this construction of theological aesthetics, I think there is an important link with feminist theology. This is found in the critique that both von Balthasar and feminist theologians have of rationalist accounts of revelation and truth and in what contexts one experiences God. My interest is in exploring this link further so as to see how it might be possible to do a feminist reading of God's beauty without the essentializing elements that polarize masculine and feminine. Feminist theologians have been drawn to the more immanent qualities of the divine: God's revealing of Godself in the beauty of nature, in childbirth, in the subtle and elusive but haunting voice of Sophia-Wisdom, and have turned to the expressions of mystical women and men for their capacity to express the divine beauty. Ideas of divine transcendence that are not dialectically related with immanence tend to place women and the feminine on the outside: the Word, speaking creation *ex nihilo*, far from the much more material conceptions of creation in the so-called 'pagan' religions. If one could sum up feminist discussions of the divine, one of the main issues would be the need to see women's experiences as evocative of the divine as much as men's. Above all, feminist theologians have discovered the beauty of God in the faces and voices of women. God's beauty is even greater than we can know, and the desire to know God in more manifestations is central.

Feminist art historians have been somewhat less shy about engaging in discussions of the aesthetic, and some of their insights may be helpful to feminist theologians. The critique of the 'male gaze' is one of the first steps in this exploration, and some recent work has emphasized how nineteenth-century ideas of the beautiful and the sublime, influenced by Kant, sought to relegate women to the 'merely' beautiful where the truly sublime was dynamic and boundless, freed from the bourgeois limitations of ornament.[25] I think that there are some analogies here to the discomfort with women's presence in liturgical settings, the historical exclusion of women's voices from choirs, with the sense that women are symbolic of the material and not of the spiritual. Feminist treatments of the aesthetic have been critical of the separation of 'art' from 'craft', as for example when the artist Judy Chicago's 'The Dinner Party', an assemblage of ceramic plates representing women, arranged in place-settings on a table, raised questions as to whether or not this constituted a work of art.[26] The focus on quilting as art is a movement which is not without precedent in the tradition-breaking practice, so to speak, of blurring the line between art and life. So to seek a feminist conception of beauty is at the same time to navigate a minefield of critiques of the role of the artist and the subject matter of art; of unhealthy ideas of female beauty, and of the role of the transcendent in life. I do not claim any proficiency in all of these debates, but I will suggest what would be significant elements in a feminist conception of beauty and how these might inform our thinking on the sacraments. The question of what beauty is is a vexing one, and here as well I cannot pretend to have covered all the bases, so to speak. But I will suggest a few elements that ought to be included. First is the recognition that beauty reveals a kind of ordering of life, or is the recognition of a kind of ordering (as in one's recognizing the 'beauty of nature'). I hesitate to use terms like 'symmetry' or 'balance' as inherent to an idea of beauty, since it is not clear to me that beauty is necessarily symmetrical or balanced. But beauty in art includes a deliberate ordering of some sort: it is a creative endeavour, and ordering is a re-arranging of the elements so as to present a new way of seeing. A feminist conception of beauty includes consideration of the ways in which the ordering of life is related to the material conditions of life (home, food, clothing) and reflection on how this ordering serves to maintain and enhance the well-being of these material conditions as well as the people they serve. I have in mind here the work done by Ndebele women in South Africa and Berber women in North Africa as documented by Margaret Courtney-Clarke.[27] Thus attention to the beauty of the home is not inappropriate here, but the focus I have in mind would serve to distinguish it from consumerist home decorating that is inattentive to the conditions of its development and maintenance. This ordering of life is related to its communal context. Second, there is a dimension of beauty that is life affirming. Here I would concur with Elaine Scarry's work *On Beauty and Being Just*, where she makes the argument that beauty is 'life-saving'. [28] The beautiful has the capacity to enlarge the vision (or hearing or other senses) of that which is presented in such a way that one comes away with a greater commitment to life, one that is done not so much from duty but joy as well. After sharing some of my ideas at a departmental colloquium, a colleague pointed me to a passage from Iris Murdoch's novel *The Bell*, where the character, Dora, has such an experience through a visit to the National Gallery: 'But the pictures were something real outside herself, which spoke to her kindly and yet in sovereign tones, something superior and good . . .'[29] After this, Dora comes to a realization about what to do with her life, a decision prompted by this experience. Such a transformation effected by art is not unusual in literature; Murdoch is but one example. Third, the beautiful is transparent to something 'more'. Scarry phrases this as the fact that beauty 'incites deliberation'.[30] The beautiful gives one pause, since one can see in it the possibility of something greater than oneself, yet it is only through that experience that one is able to come to this sense. This, I think, is the kind of contemplative sense about which von Balthasar writes and about which literature on the icon speaks. Finally, the beautiful invites and does not impose. As Scarry puts it, beauty 'incites generosity'. I put it somewhat differently here, as I have in mind the conception of beauty that Wendy Steiner describes as non-dominant and non-victimizing.

All of these dimensions are also characteristics that feminists emphasize need to be central to ideas of God. They are also very much in line with what feminist liturgists see as central to feminist ritual and sacrament: that is, our ideas of God and of liturgy need to incorporate an ordering of life that is faithful to its material conditions yet pushes us beyond it. So our conceptions of God and our liturgical celebrations must consciously recognize the conditions from which they arise. Women and men share materiality and although they may experience it differently in certain contexts, its ordering needs to be tied to the fullness of our material existence. Therefore, the relegation of women's materiality to the margins of our liturgical life does an injustice to all of our material well-being. Finally, the inviting and non-dominant quality of the beautiful mitigates against exclusionary practices and puts us in the position of responsiveness. The kind of openness, and even obedience and vulnerability, that Sarah Coakley suggests is possible for a feminist perspective, makes us more receptive to the possible graces with which we can be gifted.[31] Thinking of beauty from a feminist perspective has some potentially creative possibilities for the sacraments themselves, for our thinking about God, and for linking the sacraments more intrinsically to the work of justice in recognizing the concrete contexts of our lives.

Conclusion

To summarize my points here: first, I suggest that the issue of real presence as Chauvet envisions it is hospitable to feminist theology – indeed, more so than that of Marion. By focusing on the real presence of Christ in the community, the radical nature of the Incarnation is underscored. For Chauvet, this is the link between sacrament and justice, and I suggest that its attention to the material dimensions of human embodiment and community show a connection with feminist concerns. Second, the feminist unease with church boundary issues is not simply a signal for feminists to 'take it or leave it' when it comes to ecclesiology, nor does this suggest that boundaries are entirely irrelevant. Thus greater attention to non-eucharistic forms of spirituality and worship is indicated, first because the Eucharist cannot bear the entire burden of our liturgical life; and second, because the phenomenon of multiple religious belonging that Peter Phan and others describe is better positioned to be open to liturgical exploration. Nevertheless, feminists as well as traditionalists need to ask hard questions about the purposes of their own liturgical celebrations. Third, a feminist voice in theological aesthetics suggests a critical examination of the relation of art to materiality and otherness. Such an examination, I suggest, will enhance the relation of liturgy and sacrament to justice. The aesthetic practices of women as ways of building community and maintaining continuity offer another way to reflect on the mysterious gift of God's mysterious presence in our lives. If sacraments and sacramentality are to connect human beings to the deep mystery of God through material reality, then the experiences and insights of women must be an intrinsic dimension of this theology. Women's voices are relatively new to this conversation, but they have already raised some important questions and will continue to issue profound challenges to the discipline as well as to the sacramental life of the Christian community.

Notes

1 Susan A. Ross, *Extravagant Affections: A Feminist Sacramental Theology* (New York: Continuum Press, 1998).

2 Rosemary Radford Ruether, *Women-Church: Theology and Practice of Feminist Liturgical Communities* (Boston, MA: Beacon Press, 1985).

3 See, e.g., Lesley A. Northup, *Ritualizing Women: Patterns of Spirituality* (Cleveland, OH: Pilgrim Press, 1997); Sheila Durkin Dierks, *WomenEucharist* (Boulder, CO: Woven Word Press, 1997); Marjorie Procter-Smith and Janet R. Walton (eds), *Women at Worship: Interpretations of North American Diversity* (Louisville, KY: Westminster John Knox Press, 1993); Charlotte Caron, *To Make and Make Again: Feminist Ritual Theology* (New York: Crossroad, 1993).

4 See David R. Crownfield (ed.), *Body/text in Julia Kristeva: Religion, Women and Psychoanalysis* (Albany, NY: State University of New York Press, 1992); David N. Power has also discussed Kristeva; see his article (with R. A. Duffy and K. W. Irwin), 'Sacramental Theology: A Review of Literature,' in *Theological Studies* 55 (December 1994).

5 See Christine E. Gudorf, 'The Power to Create: Sacraments and

Men's Need to Birth', in *Horizons* 14/2, pp. 296–309 and Monika Hellwig, *The Eucharist and the Hunger of the World* (New York: Paulist Press, 1976).

6 Kathryn Tanner, 'Social Theory Concerning the "New Social Movements" and the Practice of Feminist Theology', in Rebecca S. Chopp and Sheila Greeve Davaney (eds), *Horizons in Feminist Theology: Identity, Tradition and Norms* (Minneapolis, MN: Fortress Press, 1997).

7 Jean-Luc Marion, *God Without Being*, trans. Thomas A. Carlson (Chicago, IL: University of Chicago Press, 1991); Louis-Marie Chauvet, *Symbol and Sacrament*, trans. Patrick Madigan and Madeleine Beaumont (Collegeville, MN: Liturgical Press, 1995); David N. Power, *Sacrament: The Language of God's Giving* (New York: Crossroad, 1999).

8 In 'The Otherness of God and the Bodies of Others', Theresa Sanders argues for Marion's understanding, as more adequate than Chauvet's for its focus on the Other. See *Journal of Religion* 76/4 (October 1996), pp. 572–87.

9 See Ross, *Extravagant Affections* ch. 5 (pp. 137–170) for a more extended discussion of the role of the symbolic in sacramental theology.

10 See Sanders, 'The Otherness of God', esp. p. 578.

11 Chauvet, *Symbol and Sacrament*, p. 509.

12 For an interesting Jewish perspective on Incarnation, see Elliott R. Wolfson, 'Judaism and Incarnation: The Imaginal Body of God', in Tikva Frymer-Kensky, David Novak, Peter Ochs, David Fox Sandmel and Michael A. Signer (eds), *Christianity in Jewish Terms* (Boulder, CO: Westview Press, 2000), pp. 239–54.

13 See *Chicago Tribune*, Thursday, 25 September 2003.

14 Susan A. Ross, 'A Fish Without a Bicycle?' *America 181/17* (27 November 1999), pp. 10–13.

15 See Teresa Berger, *Women's Ways of Worship: Gender Analysis and Liturgical History* (Collegeville, MN: Liturgical Press, 1999); Berger, 'Prayers and Practices of Women: *Lex Orandi* Reconfigured', in Susan K. Roll, Annette Esser and Brigitte Enzner-Probst with Charlotte Methuen and Angela Berlis (eds), *Woman, Ritual and Liturgy* (Leuven and Sterling, VA: Peeters, 2001), pp. 63–77.

16 Peter Steinfels, *A People Adrift: The Crisis of the Roman Catholic Church in America* (New York: Simon and Schuster, 2003).

17 Steinfels, *A People Adrift*, p. 282.

18 Ibid., p. 284.

19 Ibid., p. 280.

20 Ibid., p. 281.

21 Ross, 'A Fish Without a Bicycle?'

22 See Ross, *Extravagant Affections*, ch. 7, esp. pp. 204–9.

23 Peter C. Phan, 'Multiple Religious Belonging: Opportunities and Challenges for Theology and Church', *Theological Studies* 64/3 (September 2003), pp. 495–519.

24 See W. T. Dickens, *Hans Urs von Balthasar's Theological Aesthetics: A Model for Post-Critical Biblical Interpretation* (Notre Dame, IN: University of Notre Dame Press, 2003); one chapter focuses on Mary.

25 Wendy Steiner, *Venus in Exile: The Rejection of Beauty in 20th Century Art* (New York: The Free Press, 2001).

26 For a thoughtful treatment of women, art and beauty, see Wendy Steiner, *Venus in Exile: The Rejection of Beauty in 20th Century Art* (New York: The Free Press, 2001).

27 Margaret Courtney-Clarke, *Ndebele: The Art of an African Tribe* (New York: Thames and Hudson, 2002 [1986]) and *Imazighen: The Vanishing Traditions of Berber Women* (New York: Clarkson Potter, 1996).

28 Elaine Scarry, *On Beauty and Being Just* (Princeton, NJ: Princeton University Press, 1999).

29 Iris Murdoch, *The Bell* (New York, Avon Books, 1966 [1958]), p. 191.

30 Scarry, op.cit., p. 28.

31 See Sarah Coakley, *Powers and Submissions: Spirituality, Philosophy and Gender* (Oxford: Blackwell, 2002).

8

Sacred space and image as sacrament: an Indian perspective

Jyoti Sahi

Introducing art and sacramentality

Contemporary art practice seems to be returning to an earlier understanding of art processes as imbued with a ritual experience of reality. Art critical writings[1] have had a profound influence on the way that Indian artists were able to reclaim an ancient Tantric tradition in Indian art. The understanding of art as an event, rather than just as a product, can be seen in many streams of art all round the world, where the relation of art to spirituality and meditation has a new currency. And yet this rediscovery of art as an expression of an inner search for wholeness, is not without its problems for those who believe that a sacramental approach to the inner transformation of the human being should be rooted in a belief system that affirms a sense of grace, and a personal encounter with the Creator, as One whom we adore. Essential to the concept of sacrament as it is experienced in every faith system is that it provides a moment of revelation, which embodies what is eternal, beyond name and form, in that which is very physical and present in the here and now of our experience. However, it is not only embodied in the world as we experience it with our physical senses, but in that inner, subtle body which is itself a doorway into the timeless and formless. The sacrament becomes a way, through which we go beyond the physical reality to discover the spiritual in everything, freeing us from a too literal attachment to particular signs and symbols. The Christian understanding of the sacramental arises out of a belief in the Incarnation. The concept of embodiment, which seems to underlie all worldviews that see life as sacramental, remains a key concept in all efforts to relate art and the imagination to spirituality. What do we understand by 'body'? A literal approach, which looks at the body only in functional terms, or as an organism which has a centrally controlled nervous system and sensory apparatus, ignores the way in which we are constantly expanding our physical boundaries to embrace more inclusive concepts of self identity. Here the body is not limited to the way in which we perceive our own limbs, and the inner functions of what health workers see as a psychosomatic entity. We are extending our understanding of embodiment to embrace the whole environment in which we live, and the social and political networks to which we belong. To be embodied here implies incorporation into a much wider system of meanings than is the specialized world of the physician. For the artist 'body' implies form, or shape and colour. It is that which can be responded to with the human senses. It is the instrument by which we experience the world in which we live.

Institutional religion, as we find it in the structures of what we are calling Church, has perhaps understood sacramentality in a very specialized way, as defining the way in which an individual believer is incorporated into a wider body of believers. Sacraments are here taken to be steps whereby the individual not only relates to God, but also to the community. The authority to make living events into sacraments is invested in certain officially recognized persons, who are ordained to function as agents of the process of sacramentalizing spiritual experience. The very power and function of the Church as a mediator between the divine and the human depends on its authority to administer the sacraments, and so the very existence of other forms of sacramental consciousness is viewed with suspicion, as in some way inconsistent with the Church's belief in its own sacramental nature. I think that this is one of the main reasons why some church authorities view with deep concern what are considered to be alien ways of looking at the body as a sacrament, as for example in the Hindu or Buddhist understanding of yoga, which is not just a praxis of physical well being, but underlies a whole sacramentology which is to be found in an Indian worldview. In India there has been a tradition of sacred art which has viewed the work of image-making not simply as the creation of objects for worship, but as a living process which follows the different stages that characterize the evolution, realization, and final dissolution of all forms which we find underlying the rhythms of nature. The artist does not imitate nature as something external, whose appearance has to be represented, but rather as a way of drawing from those sources of energy which bring forms into being, both externally in the world of natural phenomena, and internally in the domain of human consciousness and self-awareness. Art is itself a part of nature – here conceived of within the act of perception, which is integral to all that we comprehend of creation as a cosmic event – something objective, as well as being subjective, seen and experienced by the human senses with which the body has been endowed, but also contemplated by the conscious mind and discovered in that reflective process which we call meditation. Here art and ritual are not two separate activities, the one concerned with the making of beautiful objects, the other with the worship and contemplation of these objects. Rather, the true essence of art is embodiment, the realization of forms both in terms of the creative imagination, but also as something 'given' – a grace, experienced as an inspiration that *informs* the imagination. The image is not an invention that has been conceived artificially through human skill. It is rather a form of creation, discovered within the human heart and mind, and having the power to transform the worshipper, to infuse the merely human with a power that is divine. This power transforms not only the way we see the world around us and experience the meaning of our own lives.

It transforms also the physical reality of materials as we use them; and in so doing, we ourselves are transformed by them. The human person, seen as an artist, then becomes the vessel or vehicle for a divine will that brings all things into being. Art here is itself sacramentalized, and *the image is a moment of incarnation.* The spiritual reality enters into our cultural sphere, changing the way we experience the environment in which we live.

The image as embodiment

The image as embodiment can be understood in two ways. First of all it is the way in which we realize our own bodies and the vitality that lies within our own physical being. In Indian thought, art has its inception in dance. Dance is the expression of grace as it is found within the body. But there is another embodiment that is contained in our experience of clothing, shelter and environment – what we could call the inhabited space as understood by the Greek term *oikos*, or Sanskrit terms like *Sthana, Loka,* or *Jagat.* Perhaps we could speak of these concepts in terms of place, that is, space localized in the here and now, embodied in the context of a living or inhabited space. It is in this context that I would like to explore the idea of image not just as something made, but something entered into, made one's own in the process of finding one's own body, as in a movement, or a gesture which both communicates and celebrates – with space as the theatre of that movement, the arena of that manifestation. The ancient master craftspeople, who constructed the image or the sacred building, were known in the south of India as *Acharis,* that is, those competent in an established skill. They were carpenters, in that the Creator of the Universe or *Vishva Karma* (*Pantocrator,* to use the Greek term, *vishva* being the 'whole world', and *karma* being the 'work' of creation) was thought of as a carpenter. He fashions the stage out of the wood of the Tree of Life, joins things together like a wheelwright, but is also a master ritualist, knowing the right times and seasons in which the work is to be accomplished in harmony with the rhythms of the cosmos. According to the 'competent ones' the building, or image as *murti*, is the embodiment of ultimate *space* in present *time*. The place of the image is like the primal feminine principle, the *Shakti*, or energy to which the image or built space is married, as the husband joined to the wife. To join, in this deeply spiritual sense, is a *yoga*, a word derived from *yuj*, to bring together, to yoke or conjugate, as in the conjugal act of marriage. Sri Aurobindo referred to this as Integral Yoga, and pointed out that it is not only an ascent, as in the concept of attaining to higher states of being; it is also a descent, a way of going into the very material reality of the opaque world in which we live. E. B. Havell[2] refers to a Buddhist Tantric text which seems to outline what one might call a Divine Office for artists. Here art begins with a moment of visualization. The art practice entails finding a suitable place and sitting in that place in meditation. The mind is left open, ready to receive the insight, which comes not from within, but as something poured into the human vessel from outside. The first step is thus a deep effort at self-emptying, of cleansing the vessels of thought. Then the spirit is invoked, and this is the essence of what we are to understand by *mantra*. Invocation is a work of harmonization, of discovering the cosmic sound, which permeates the whole of creation as AUM, the primal utterance of the Divine Word. This gradually becomes visible, as a kind of light, and moves on to be embodied. The image now takes shape in the imagination of the one who meditates. The artist as a celebrant of this mystery now makes various intentions: self-offering by asking the image to enter into, become part of the artist's sensory world, then welcoming, then prostrating before this mysterious Other. The artworker, or instrument of this act of embodiment, then offers the present creation to the whole cosmos, intending that what has here been realized should not be for the possession of any individual, but should be for the ultimate liberation of the whole universe, and the help of every creature (a prominent theme in Buddhist faith). Finally, having created this visible and tangible form as a sacrament of the creative power that has given birth to the whole creation, it is necessary for the art worker to go further and to realize that all this is ultimately no-thing. Into the 'fire of emptiness', the maker thus consigns all manifest works, realizing that dissolution is finally speaking the ultimate state of all that is envisioned, in the sense of re-membered. It is only through this final meditation on the transparency, or impermanence of all that we experience as phenomena, that the artist, along with the worshipper, is able to go beyond the image and to realize that which is imageless within the image. It is in this formless dimension of all form that the ultimate transformation of the inner person is effected.

In this Tantric exercise we also realize that the artist is only an instrument, and that art is something very impermanent and very conditional. Always when discussing the sacramental, we are concerned with two elements, with what is archetypal, cosmic, universal, and what is localized, and in that sense accidental. It is this central issue that the Indian Jesuit theologian Michael Amaladoss addressed in a book concerned with questions of 'inculturation'.[3] For the last thirty-five years I too have been involved in a movement in the Indian Church, which has tried to understand how the liturgical life and practice of the Church can be comprehended from an Indian perspective. This is not just a question of how we can adapt Christian sacraments to an Indian cultural milieu; how, for example, we can create an Indian Rite or an Indian Anaphora. We have to go beyond the outer forms to address a far more fundamental question: how has India understood *sacrament* itself, and sacramental life as integrated in the very web of cultural practice? Here we are not dealing only with external dressing, or decorations, but with the very notion of sacramentality in the context of another civilization. What is it to make an image, and to believe that this image has the power to transform and sacramentalize the world in which we live?

Sacrament as celebrating the mystery

The word *sacramentum* is of course itself a Latin term, originally applying to the vow taken by soldiers in the Roman legions. Thus *sacramentum* implied a deposit, or surety in the sense of a sacred commitment, a solemn obligation. It could also mean something laid down, and in that sense also carried the sense of a sacred place or *temenos*, a place cut off, kept safe. In fact that would also have been one of the root meanings of *sacer*, from which the very word sacred comes, from the root *sa*, that which is saved. The Sanskrit word *sarva*, meaning whole, probably also comes from this root meaning. It was Augustine who gave this term *sacramentum* an ecclesial meaning, referring, for example, to Baptism as a sacrament. The question we may ask is how this notion of sacrament relates to the world of mystery, which is also a basic coefficient of the liturgy. The sacrament implied something public, whereas the mystery was hidden. The sacrament as a vow, or public commitment, was something manifest, whereas the mystery was essentially that which cannot be revealed. Perhaps here we are touching on another important distinction between the 'sacred' and the 'holy'. There has been a discussion, in relation to the Ashram movement in India, about the importance on the one hand of liturgy, or a public or community ritual, and on the other hand meditation and yoga. The Hindu understanding of the *samskaras*, often referred to as Hindu sacraments, relates to an inner process of transformation. The root (literally, 'making together', 'composing') is the same as that for both Sanskrit language and culture (*sanskrita*). This process of transformation is compared to the slow effort that goes into the polishing of something rough or unfinished. So, it is a process of refinement, with the *samskaras* as a series of rites of passage, which follow the individual from the moment of conception to the final dissolution of the body in death. Similarly, the *ashramas* were originally the stages of life that every person is required to pass through on the journey leading from youthful formation (*brahmachari*) through household commitments (*grihastha*) to a time when duties are relinquished, and the individual sets out in search of deeper and more spiritual goals (*vanaprastha*), culminating in the complete stripping away of all external responsibilities (*sanyasa*). This path towards self-realization may have its public vows and even social contracts, which might help in ensuring a serious commitment to this inner effort of self-perfection.

However, the ultimate purpose of this spiritual way is an inner mysterious destiny, with its own compulsions which sometimes cannot even be defined or articulated.

This inner spiritual destiny is distinct from the identities which religious formalism imposes on individuals and groups; it points beyond sacraments to a realization of the whole sacramentality of life itself. While it is seemingly impossible to make this journey without particular sacramental acts as public events, sacraments and their imagery can so easily degenerate into merely outward forms or rituals. How can we discover that deep consciousness of the holy in life as a whole? The increasing tendency to secularization in our modern rationalistic and profane society has, among other things, been seen as a threat to those sacred institutions whose very power or influence on the community has rested on the administration of sacraments. Now as fewer people feel the need to baptize their children as a sign of their identity within and belonging to a faith, or to get married in a church, or finally to have their mortal rest in a clearly defined Christian graveyard, it would appear that the very foundations of what we are calling Church is under threat. Even the word 'spiritual' is often viewed in church circles with some misgivings, as if it implied an alternative way to ecclesial belonging. The power of the priest, or the institutional Church, has often rested on the exclusive right of the ordained to determine what is sacramental and what is not. In this way sacraments have often become instrumentalized as the prerogative of an official church body that is also recognized by the state. As a counter to this tendency I have four further points to make.

1. Sacramentality and embodiment

First, we should think of *sacramentality as a crucially important way of healing*. When we speak of image and space as sacramental we are looking at a spiritual dimension of reality. For, with the sacramental we are concerned with the whole process of embodiment. It is here that liturgical action is very different from meditation. Neither, though, should be seen as of a higher order than the other. Rather, each needs the other. Liturgy enacts the mystery and in that way embodies the spiritual; meditation moves beyond action, into the pure world of contemplative experience. Thus, contemplation goes beyond the image, to find the mystery of the imageless. It is like the space in which the image is unfolded, but it is not that image. The image, however, has to have a form, a body. And yet, as we remarked earlier, image is married to space. Without space, image has no life, no power to transform. In the same way liturgy which does not lead on to meditation becomes meaningless rubric. It is in this movement into meditation that takes us beyond the image that we rediscover the importance of healing. Healing is about the body, but it is also an affirmation of wholeness, and hence of holiness. The distinction we might draw between the holy and the sacred is necessary if we are to understand the relation of the sacramental rites to spiritual healing. True healing is not just a physical state; it also involves the mind, the soul, the way in which we are conscious of our own bodies, and are able to integrate the physical with the spiritual within our lives. The problem with much modern medicine is that it is related to a technology, a tremendous advance in a scientific understanding of how the body functions, but it is not really concerned with healing. That is why all kinds of alternative therapies have become very important to people: they represent a longing for a deeper wisdom about the body which includes the spiritual dimension. This desire for wholeness is also part of what we are now trying to find in a sacramentalized view of reality.

What we might find in the Hindu approach to sacrament-like *samskaras*, is an understanding of life processes which are related to a cosmic worldview. The human body is a microcosm, and so the various stages of its growth, the day-to-day rhythms that govern its functions, are related to a much wider scheme of nature, which extends to the whole cosmos. What the *samskaras* bring to the consciousness of the individual is the way in which the body does not separate us from a much wider, all-inclusive body, but is rather the threshold to the cosmos. We discover the cosmos in our own bodies. I believe that one of the most important insights which Indian religions bring to our understanding of the Incarnation is the realization that the body of Christ is not simply historically or geographically conditioned, but is in fact a cosmic body. The liturgy, and indeed the various mysteries which the liturgy enacts, are all pointers to this cosmic body of the Lord. The elements of the sacrament are not just a remembrance of what Jesus did in the flesh, when he was born and lived amongst his disciples two thousand years ago. The elements are also windows, which open our vision on to the deeper significance of the whole universe in which we live. It is in that sense that we can speak of the sacramental elements as archetypal and the eucharistic elements of bread and wine as entry points into a deeper awareness of the very substance of all matter, focusing our attention on the way in which the whole earth is caught up in the self-offering of Christ on the Cross. The Indian Anaphora[4] tries to situate the Eucharist within this cosmic vision. What is important is not whether wine or bread is essential but that the Eucharist enables us to experience our bodies as part of this greater body of the whole universe, and that this sacrament recalls us to a deeper spiritual communion with the whole world.

It is perhaps in this context that we have to review the vexed problem taken up by Michael Amaladoss.[5] So often the debate on what can or cannot be inculturated can become wrapped up in all kinds of insignificant details. Inculturation seems to be a problem of cosmetics, or stage management, as though the important question in putting on a drama were the make-up of the actors, their costumes, and various properties of the stage. In fact, the true action, which the drama unfolds, goes beyond these props, however important they are in the actual task of performance. When we talk about embodiment we are of course speaking of the here and now, this particular place and time. Bodies are temporal, as also are temples. Cultures do not exist in the abstract. They have been created by communities who have interacted with their natural environment. The geography of a particular region, its climate and physical features, has definitely helped to create what we might call a local culture. But what we call a civilization goes beyond these limited features which have given rise to a culture in the first place. Indian civilization extends far beyond the Indian subcontinent. There are those who live far away from India who have been profoundly influenced by Indian civilization and by the faith systems which have arisen out of this civilization. Thus Buddhism, which began in India, is hardly to be found (except in very recent *Dalit* movements) as a living faith in the India that we know today. Yet its influence is felt in every aspect of Indian culture, and it has also profoundly affected the beliefs of people far away from India, right across Asia, and now increasingly in Europe and the Americas. The same is also true of Christianity. Christianity, beginning in Palestine, was formed within the context of a largely Aramaic culture. Yet the Palestine we know today has only a few Christians who belong there. Christianity also has gone through many changes, and has been absorbed into faraway cultures, which have little in common, culturally speaking, with the world into which the historical Jesus was born.

2. *The search for the oriental Christ*

My second point concerns the *search for the Oriental Christ*. At one level, this has been an effort to imagine Jesus from an Indian point of view, not as a European figure, but more as a wisdom teacher of the far East, a storyteller or even folk healer of the kind we are familiar with wandering the pilgrim roads. Christian iconography has been based on a system known as 'typology', which seems to go back to Jesus himself, as found in a number of narratives of Luke, where his ministry is presented in the light of certain Old Testament types. Later, this typology was extended by the gentile Church, which discovered 'types of Christ' in such pre-Christian figures as Orpheus, or even certain philosophers of the Greek tradition, as Paul proposed in his famous speech given in Athens. In India we might find other 'types' of Christ, as in the figure of the *Lord of the Dance*, or the image of '*Iswara*' in the famous *Trimurti* image of the Elephanta caves. There was a definite tendency amongst certain early missionaries to India, before the ninth century, to see Jesus as a new Buddha, and it is possible that elements of this Christology influenced the lamaistic art along the silk route to the Far East. This tendency to imagine Jesus walking on the dusty roads of India gained new impetus as a result of the efforts to translate the Bible, particularly the New Testament, into the languages of the Orient. We can trace the emergence of an Indian image of Jesus to the creative work of reformed Hindus who found in the New Testament, now available in translation, a compelling figure, whom they could easily imagine in the robes of a Hindu or Buddhist ascetic. Subsequently other types emerged, more connected with those who had been oppressed by the caste system: Jesus the tribal prophet, or the Dalit 'Suffering Servant'. I have been trying to explore these various images of Jesus as a possible contribution to an Asian Christology, where visual representations have been as important as written texts. The *murti* in Hindu tradition is itself a sacrament. The image is not merely a help to the imagination, but is a real presence, to have a vision of whom is the ultimate goal of the pilgrim. Those who come to the Temple come for a *darshana*, that is, a 'vision' of the Lord as present in the holy of holies. I would like to extend this concept of the face of the Lord to a more abstract notion of the Holy Land, an interior landscape which is the body of God as discovered in and through our experience of the natural environment in which we live. The cosmic face of Christ is no more simply 'anthropomorphic' than it is 'pantheistic'. Christ is a Person whose presence is not only found in our fellow human beings, but also in the elemental world in which we live. We need to discern the features of Christ in the very natural elements that constitute our planet earth. Here the sacramental image becomes aniconic, including the whole of nature. Earlier we introduced the idea of the 'imageless image'. This of course appears to be a contradiction in terms, rather like speaking of the nothing which is in every thing. But if we understand by 'nothing' a space, and we recognize the image as a thing, an object which exists inside a space, then we realize that the image needs space in order to unfold and become the entity which it is, in the same way that the *Tao Te Ching* says that the pot needs a space inside it, if it is to be useful, or the room needs the space which it contains, if it is to be habitable. The image always needs the space, which is not an image, in order to be alive, and a place where the imagination can rest. We find that in so many of the sacramental forms which use images, the image is created, honoured as the object of devotion, but then allowed to return to that world of non-image from which it originally came into being. I believe that for a form to become sacramental, it must include this dimension of no-form, or formlessness. This is an important aspect of all acts of worship, which we find, even at a very elemental and popular level, in India. For example, when the festival of Ganesh, a very popular folk deity, comes in the season of growth and life, during the time of the monsoon in India, the image is created out of clay, which has been taken from a village reservoir or tank. The clay is moulded into the form of this earth god, who symbolizes in many ways the living force which we find in the elemental. After the figure is completed, a festival lasting many days takes place, because Ganesh is the god of culture, of story telling, dancing, and music. After the celebration is over, the figure is carried in procession by the whole community, and immersed again in the waters of the reservoir from which he was taken as the clay body, which was used to mould his form. This ritual destruction of the image is part of the sacramental life of the image. The image is not permanent – it is only provisional. It is given to human beings as a focus for the imagination, but ultimately it is returned to the matrix of nature, from which it was originally drawn.

What Michael Amaladoss argues, using the philosophical discipline of semiology, is that the sacrament is always a 'sign' which points to a reality that it 'signifies', and that we need to understand better the way in which signs function within the symbol system of a given culture, if we are to reflect on the power which sacraments have in our lives. The great Indian thinker Shankara Acharya, who lived in the ninth century and developed that system of thought called *Advaita*, 'non-dualism', believed that we can only properly deal with the ultimate meaning of things by way of *lakshana-artha*. *Lakshana* means 'sign', 'indication', and invariably 'indirect sign'. *Artha* can connote 'meaning', but here probably just means 'by way of'. Like the Buddhist epistemologists, Shankara makes much of the idea that the finger which points is not the same as that to which it points. In this context, in giving the example of the bridegroom who points to a star in the sky – as is required in a Hindu marriage ceremony – the great Advaitin goes further. The star that has to be pointed out is actually rather a faint, difficult star to see. It is called the *Arundhati* star and is supposed to be the faithful wife of the seven sages, who form what is known in the West as the Plough, part of the constellation of the Great Bear. In order to identify this star, the teacher first points out another, more obvious constellation. 'It is not that one', the teacher explains, 'but from there look . . .' So, gradually, one sign leads to another sign which in its turn is then dismissed, until finally the desired star is discovered and seen. The whole sky is a vast system of star-signs. To read this system, our gaze is lead by the pointing hand of the teacher. What is pointed out cannot be seen directly even though it is present in the vast spaces of the sky. Images are pointers, but what they point to lies beyond our ability to imagine.

3. The garden temenos

Then thirdly, there is *the garden temenos as sacramental space*. In the India of today sacred places of worship in the form of built spaces, be they temples, mosques or churches, often become the occasion for bitter contentions, as different religious groups claim proprietary rights over sacred sites. In this context the very walls, which have been constructed around holy places, become signs of division. In the context of the Indian Church, there has been a growing perception amongst tribal *Adivasi* ('first inhabitants') or *Dalit* (literally 'broken') converts to Christianity, that the built-up forms of the Hindu temple, however meaningful as architectural concepts, have represented for them no-go areas, where they have been denied access because of their perceived status as ritually impure communities. The term outcaste has its specific meaning as referring to those individuals who, by virtue of the fact that they belong to certain non-Aryan communities, have been perceived by the high caste as polluting and therefore have not been allowed into their sacred precincts. As a consequence the temple has been associated with a religious system which, for those who have been debarred from access to these ritual places, has come to represent all that is repressive and alienating. On this account, the very form of these places of worship and the rituals performed in them have come to be rejected by those who were not allowed to enter these sacred spaces. In this context, aboriginal communities have wanted to return to their *Ur*-symbols, primordial signs of identity related to the open countryside in which they have been nomads, people without any settled habitation. For these people the God of the Old Testament, who was a guiding Presence, unrestricted to the cult of a particular place, but a wanderer, sharing the exile of a displaced people, has been particularly meaningful. The Sanskrit word *ambara*, meaning a shaded or sheltered place, may well be etymologically linked to the Latin *umbra*, or shadow, from which the word umbrella is also derived. In a monograph on the superstructure which defines the sacred space of the temple, Ananda Coomaraswamy points out that the Hindu temple has evolved from a primordial worship of holy trees, under whose branches were located shrines which were often linked to rites of fertility. These shrines were gradually protected by the built area of the *temenos*, starting with a raised platform and then slowly evolving into a covered area with pillars, and finally an enclosing wall to define that which lies within from the outside profane world. Great sages like those we find described in the Upanishads, also called *aranyakas* (meaning 'belonging to the forest'), or *aranya*, were pictured as sitting under the outstretched branches of sacred trees like the peepul tree, or *ficus religiosa*, or again the banyan tree, or some other tree which is thought to be a tree of healing or wisdom. The Buddha himself received enlightenment whilst sitting under such special trees of life and knowledge and later taught his first disciples in the sacred grove of Sarnath on the banks of the River Ganges near the present-day holy city of Varanasi, or Benares. Thus the sage is sometimes referred to, especially in the Jaina tradition, as *Dig-ambara*, or clothed in space. Temples like the great Chidambara in south India, where Nataraja, the Lord of the Dance, is supposed to dance in the *sanctum sanctorum*, itself referred to as the *Linga,* or seed-bearing Pillar of Space, was again probably at one time a sacred grove where, as in the tribal *akhara* or open space beneath the branches of a tree, the ritual of the sacred dance was performed.

The architect Laurie Baker, with whom I worked for some years when I was closely associated with the ashram of Dom Bede Griffiths, often stressed the importance of open spaces in Indian built-up places, such as the enclosed courtyard, or temple tank within the cloistered interior of the temple complex. The mosque has also developed such interior spaces, which are used for congregational worship, especially suited to the warm and sunny climate of Asia. Why should the oriental Church follow the model of those enclosed buildings, which are suitable in a cold and northern climate, but are hardly appropriate for the weather conditions of the Orient? As a result Laurie Baker tried to incorporate into his church designs interior gardens into which worshippers could spread out especially on feast days, when many people are gathered together and the covered area around the sanctuary becomes insufficient to house everyone. In this way we can begin to envisage a sacred space, which returns to the prototype of the holy grove, the garden that is both a place to relax in, but also to meditate on the presence of God in creation. Here the divine mystery is once again re-discovered in the fertile land, which lies open to the skies. We need to rediscover the holy in the landscape, not cut off from the elemental forces of nature. Gandhi, echoing the sentiments of the poet Rabindranath Tagore, said that he wanted his place of worship to be open on every side, but not so open that the winds come and blow it down. It is this balance of openness to enclosure that we are trying to rediscover in our understanding of the sacramental in life.

4. The image as sadhana

Finally, there is *the image as sadhana*. I began this reflection by saying that in the thought of India art is not just a skill concerned with the making of objects, however beautiful, but is essentially a way of life. Coomaraswamy is said to have coined the aphorism, repeated also by Eric Gill, that the artist is not a special sort of person, but every person is a special sort of artist. To be human, every person has to find within himself or herself the talent that is the source of their own special form of creativity. The human person is made in the image of God, inasmuch as we are called in some mysterious measure to be co-creators of the world in which we live. This responsibility to participate in the continuing process of bringing creation to birth is the priestly function of every believer. It is on this all-inclusive assumption that a theology of art has to be founded. It is in this context that Indian aesthetics is essentially interactive. Some of India's outstanding philosophers, such as M. Hiriyanna (who was a teacher of Radhakrishna), have argued that art is not a work, so much as an experience. He suggests, in his essay on the quest for perfection, that there is no real term for beauty in Indian philosophy, for the search for beauty as 'Saundary' in Vedantic thought is always subsumed under the general concern for human values and the longing for that which is the ultimate goal of life. Goodness, according to Indian aesthetics, cannot be divorced from the beautiful, as though the good of the work can be distinguished from the good of life. In this context the statement of the aestheticians, characterized by the aphorism of Oscar Wilde that 'the fact that a man is a poisoner is nothing against his prose', becomes senseless. Ultimately speaking, argues Hiriyanna, the art experience is *Brahma vidya*, or knowledge of God as Brahman. The joy that is evoked by that which is pleasing to the senses is nothing other than the joy of the spirit, *ananda*. It is insights such as these which could enrich a Christian understanding of art and the search for beauty as an essential coefficient of what we are calling the sacramental. We do need to free our understanding of the sacramental from the rigid institutionalism of religious ritual, which, like the walls that divide places of worship, sets up barriers between people of good faith. The sacramental should be essentially the discovery of the mystery of communion, the celebration of our common journey towards a reaffirming of the divine presence in creation. That is why a theology of creation, or an eco-theology, is essential for a new way of looking at art as itself sacramental. The divine image and its relation to holy space must become once again the sign of culture in search of human values, and not as the venue for the so-called 'clash of civilizations'. To rediscover this we need to get out of built forms, to find once again the spiritual, which informs our ritual's open spaces.

Notes

1 See, for example, Ajit Mookerjee, *Ritual Art of India* (London: Thames and Hudson, 1986).
2 See E. B. Havell, 'Ideals of Indian Art', in his work *The Art Heritage of India* (Bombay: D. B. Taraporevala & Sons, 1964).
3 M. Amaladoss, *Do Sacraments Change? Variable and Invariable Elements in Sacramental Rites* (Bangalore: Theological Publications in India, 1979).
4 *An original Eucharistic Prayer for India*, available from the National Biblical, Liturgical and Catechetical Centre, Bangalore.
5 Amaladoss, *Do Sacraments Change?*

9

Sacrament: the poetics of justification

David N. Power OMI

In interpreting 'symbols, texts and practices' of ecclesial traditions,[1] it is a matter of common persuasion that a primary location for the reception and faith interpretation of scriptures and key symbols is the assembly for worship. Therein diverse scriptural texts are intertwined in proclamation, and scriptural narratives and scriptural root metaphors are worked into sacramental prayers. While there is an interaction of actions, words, visual representations and sounds, in this paper the focus is placed on the word of prayer, which is here called the poetic word. This poetic word of blessing is related to the four basic sacramental things of bread, wine, oil and water. The word expresses the sense that is given to the sacramental as a memorial of God's action for the world in Christ, his Son and Word, and in the Spirit. As memorial, sacrament is itself a continuous action in the Spirit of God's eternal and loving election, justification and new creation, related to the time-determined human realities evoked in the elements and in their communal participation. The images of justification are here evoked because our world stands ever in need of the merciful and justifying act of God. As churches turn to God in prayer they share the distress whereby our time suffers a loss even of the power of language, to evoke reality, to express meaning, to encourage hope. This affects all uses of language but in a particular way challenges the confidence of religious language. All kinds of questions are raised about the legitimacy of certain expressions, about the referents of discourse, about the possibility of finding meaning in words and, of course, beyond that in life. When this is however linked to a passion for justice and peace, it may be seen as a delivery of language usage from ideologies and as a liberation of the power of words to generate new meanings within standing traditions. To generate new meaning, the shifts in the significance of words require some 'death of meaning' and hence a death of being, a death to being, and in this a necessary surrender to death itself. This is the way of being in life and in history. Paradoxically, a future is to be found in living through the death of meaning, with courage and with care, and with a passion for caring for the suffering, for those who are the victims of ideological interests embedded in systems of symbols, systems of speaking, and in the economic and political systems which they support. Unhappily, many of our memories that mark the twentieth century are painful and troubling but get left out of sacramental action, which may be too closed within itself to give them entry. Hence, there are four points in what I have to say here. First, I explain why talking of the poetics of justification is a good sacramental heuristic. This is then illustrated by looking at the poetics of eucharistic memorial in several traditions. Third, I relate poetics to an understanding of justification as divine act. Fourth, I make some suggestions for the retrieval of sacramental poetics through a renewed sense of sacramental action as expression of the living Body of Christ and through a poetic employ of living metaphors.

Poetics of justification as heuristic

Speaking of the *poetics of justification*, a heuristic is being employed of sacramental celebration as a language event.[2] The event of Christ's Pasch events anew in a community through sacramental discourse, in all its components. The heuristic accounts for bringing together into the memorial of Christ the proclamation of the Word, the word of doxological prayer and the offer of a gift announced through the elements of creation, bread, wine, oil and water. It allows us to take into account the contours of words heard or spoken in the community, with its great diversity of types of discourse and its constant creative capacity for expressing meaning. It also attends to the particularities of experience, history and culture. Gathering in the Spirit to keep memorial and moved by the prophetic inspiration of the Spirit, churches are endowed with their reality as the Body of Christ in a time-encrusted way, respectful of peoples and of cultures. In keeping memorial, the Church is mindful that Christ himself is given to us as Saviour in word event. There would be no vision of the Crucified One as Saviour, if he and those who proclaimed him had not found their place in an already existing language memory. He can be celebrated as Saviour because of the place he is shown to have in a much longer story, in prevision of a coming judgement. To bring the story remembered and lived to fulfilment, Jesus' own submission to death was an emptying-out which, in order to allow God's mercy its fullness, meant a death to a closure of meanings that prevented a vision of the future. What he lived through in dying, his disciples must live through in his being embodied in them by Spirit.

Poetics

Why talk then of poetics? The term is used here in order to respect but move beyond what has been ecumenically established by a liturgical and theological emphasis on *anamnesis* and *epiclesis*. This attention has allowed us to acknowledge that all ecclesial worship is done in the Spirit and that what we do is a memorial and representation of what God has done in Christ, once and for all. However, at times it results in a failure to reflect more fully on those parts of blessing prayers outside the texts technically called by these two names. We affirm in faith what is being done, but what meaning do prayers construe in their use especially of biblically metaphoric language? While poetry 'presses back against the pressures of reality', as Seamus Heaney has it,[3] it also breaks with the everyday, with commonplace

147

ways of looking at this reality. It breaks us free, relating the moment caught to something more profound and launches the hearer into some desired future that is not so entrapped as 'the day that is in it', to use an Irish colloquialism. While poetics as a doing with language is not confined to the poem in a strict sense, this may serve as an ideal model on which to base further semantic study. Of its nature it is exploratory and innovative, even while working with a language and a memory that it supposes known to its readers and hearers. However, the dictionary and cultural lore, while they must be consulted, fail to explain the meaning of poetry. It is grasped only in its metaphorical shifts and displacements, whatever its recognizable allusions. Since this same reflective and conative stance occurs in other forms of expression as well, namely the symbolic, the visual, the ritual, the term *poetic* may be extended to embrace the exploration of what they do by way of disjunctive signification and innovative signification. Where the ritual scores as bodily action, and as that bodily action with things, is in conscribing the being in time of those addressed and which poetry respects, even as it presses against them. Released from excessive rigidity, core actions such as washing and eating and drinking in the very intensity of their rhythm bring to the surface the sense of a hazardous being in time and space and the tensions inherent to the human condition. They therefore construe a human and cosmically aware environment in which the word may be heard, received and spoken. Ideology may indeed impose a rigid control over things and actions but by quiet innovations in ritual performance the power of the symbolic exchange is broken open. Those who take are invited to be open to what can be received only as gift and to take on new shapes in living a community life whose divine expression is the oneness of all without differentiation at the common table. The poetic of openness to the transcendent – to mystery – is already there, but, when keeping memorial of Christ in word and song culminates at that point, what is daily revealed is the mystery of God's own self-giving as the foundation for our being one, and our being one with all of creation.

The poetic diction of eucharistic prayers

The power of the poetic of discourse needs to be recovered from a hermeneutical study of liturgical traditions. Given the limits of time and space, by way of an example, these remarks are restricted to the Eucharist simply to pinpoint the diversity in poetic construal of a few traditions. In doing this, we may be attentive both to the way in which Christ is remembered and to the way in which eschatological hope is expressed. To start, one may compare two early anaphoras, those of *Addai and Mari* and of the *Apostolic Tradition*.[4] The former is still used today among Chaldeans and East Syrians. Since it is without the Supper Narrative it has often been mangled by scholars and spurned by authorities. However, this is now accepted even by Rome as a thoroughly respectable prayer and one that can be given complete eucharistic value. I will not go into the subtleties of curial explanation but the absence of an explicitly evoked Supper Narrative gives fresh perception to how we celebrate in memory and look forward in hope, not simply repeating some ancient words. Concerns over the causality of the words of the Lord or of the *epiclesis* respectively may be set aside and the focus put on a prayer's ability to give expression to a community's act of recreative remembering, to its recasting of the story with prophetic and doxological utterance, to its contemplation of the mystery. Heard in this way, through its poetic language, a prayer of blessing opens the ear, the eye and the mouth to the event of the Crucified and Risen One in its midst and to the gift he offers.

In the prayer of *Addai and Mari*, it is the coming into the world, the taking on flesh by God's beloved Son which is seen as the truly wondrous and creative moment of salvation. The death may indeed be inevitable but it is the enfleshment that catches attention, the kind of thing indeed that was repeatedly evoked in the doctrinal battles between Nestorius and Cyril over who Jesus truly is in the flesh. Thanks is given because the Son in his human flesh 'brought about a great grace which cannot be repaid'. Putting on a human nature, he 'raised us from our lowly

149

state', 'restored our Fall . . . our immortality', 'forgave us our debts . . . justified our sinfulness . . . enlightened our intelligence'. Though the prayer is honoured in communities who hold Nestorius in regard, we can also find its imagery in other authors. In Athanasius and Cyril of Alexandria the Incarnation is seen as a taking on of struggle, of combat, a readiness to face the evil that abounds in the world to conquer it by giving of self in love. In the prayer it may also be noted that in its *exordium* it relates this wondrous event of divine enfleshment back to the eternal mystery. It is the revelation in time of the all-holy name of Father, Son and Spirit. Those who pray are placed standing in awe before the holiness of God, revealed in the flesh of the Son's combat with the forces of death. Though the prayer in the *Apostolic Tradition* has the Supper Narrative, it is not meant to stand apart from the rest of the prayer. It is in effect the act in which the Son anticipates the consummation of his life when, extending his arms in suffering, he broke death itself. In the act of remembering, both here and in the Liturgy of Basil, what is celebrated is how Christ, the Word through whom God made the universe, by his cross overcomes death, sin, the powers of darkness, to enter into the resurrection that is intended for all flesh. Basil, in an adroit fashion, subsumes this image and the whole Christ story under the image of *kenosis*. Moreover, by placing at the Baptism of the Son, this 'citizen of the world', the adjoinment to himself of a holy people, a royal priesthood, he is represented as carrying this with him into the torments of his passion and the descending among the dead, and so into the rising of his flesh. In the need to be brief, the third example of poetic creativity is taken from Reformation worship, and specifically from Martin Luther. His creative contribution to creative memory comes through the renewal of proclamation, the renewal of ritual actions of communion, and through hymns, and to a lesser extent through certain prayers for liturgical worship, such as that for Baptism. As we know, Luther wished to have the faithful hear the Supper Narrative, in which he found the testament of the Lord to the forgiveness of sins and divine mercy. He also wished the ritual actions of eating and drinking to be restored and to be seen both as the gift of the body and blood of the Saviour and as the seal of the eschatological promise. It should not be forgotten, either, that he wanted his brethren to remain in awe of the wonder and holiness of the One who saves, and so asked that Communion be accompanied by the singing of the German *Sanctus*. Finally he composed hymns which in a poetic way expressed the meaning of memorial when the accent is placed on the justification by Christ's grace of sinful humanity. His use of biblical metaphors stands out for example in the eucharistic hymn, *Christus lag in Todesbanden*,[5] wherein Luther retrieves the imagery of conflict between life and death, goodness and malice, as in song he accompanies the congregants to the paschal chalice and to the meat of Christ's body.

On the base of these few examples, we see that liturgical traditions are in fact constantly and imaginatively recasting the memory of Christ and the projection of salvation in which humankind hopes. They do this by their selection, by their intertextualizing of scriptural texts to be proclaimed and by the way in which they integrate scriptural metaphors and narratives into doxology. In effect, these innovative poetic traditions give us different theologies, where theology is the word of God, God through Spirit and the remembrance of God adventing in our midst. It is in this eventing, made corporeal in the things of earth and in culturally rooted communities with their own histories, that God comes in the living memory of Christ and in the power of a Spirit that makes this possible. Given half a chance, Christian communities on the continents of Africa and Asia are doing the same thing today, though Western vigilance is sometimes too strong to allow them free rein.

Justification

The example of Luther's liturgies of course brings our attention back to the issue of justification, which this paper intentionally highlights. Between Lutheran and Catholic, between Orthodox and Lutheran, between Anglican and Lutheran, much advance has been made in settling disputes over what is meant by justification by faith. In all cases this is accomplished by return to what Christ has done for humankind by his death and by adverting to how much sinful mortals depend on Christ and the gift of his Spirit in their journey towards God. In the agreement between the Anglican and Lutheran communities, the Porvoo Statement[6] places the doctrine in a clearly liturgical setting, which in essence means an invitation to place justification by faith within a context of keeping sacramental memorial. If this is done, the question of human salvation and justification and the invitation to a saving faith is placed within the dynamic of trinitarian action. Faith is elicited within the creative celebration of the Church's sacramental action, whether in the washing with water, the anointing by the Spirit or the communion in the gifts offered us at the eschatological table. As a poetics of justification, sacrament exacts of us that we retrieve the vocabulary of justice and justification as well as of eschatological hope from the Scriptures themselves, but in a creative way. Only a few brief remarks are here possible.[7] As Paul writes of justification in Romans and Galatians, what is first and foremost at issue is God's election of the people with whom he makes covenant and the total gratuity of this election. The language of Paul is that of the *dikaiosyne* of God, of justice, of righteousness, of God making just those who have no claim to being justified. This God has done through Christ who offered himself as sacrifice for sin, who became sin, who emptied himself, who thus overcame sin and death.[8] Conscious of what God has done in Christ, he works with the tradition handed down through the Law and the Prophets. The faith, moreover, whereby the elect are justified is the work of the Spirit and with justification there goes the gift of the Spirit who enables believers to love God as Father and teaches them how they ought to pray. Thus the language of justification is inseparable from the language of sanctification in the Spirit and from that of reconciliation, this latter of great moment when even in the efforts to make global community we experience division, hatred, intolerance, oppression and injustice. There is also judgement from which to be delivered, but it is the eschatological judgement, the judgement made at the end of time when under the loving eye of God and in respect of the saving death of the Son, life and death are definitively separated. Life endures, but those who have lived by the rule of injustice and death shall be dead forever. It is from this judgement that the justice of Christ delivers those who live by faith in him and in the mercy shown in him.

We can enrich this language by an appeal to Matthew's Gospel. In the preaching of Jesus in Matthew about the reign of God we find brought together with justice and associated with Jesus himself such covenant expressions as kingdom or reign, God's merciful will for us, perfection of holiness and bearing fruit by heeding to this reign of God. The language of reign becomes an encompassing term but it has a dependent meaning, making it necessary to recall the significance of the Davidic dynasty for Israel and its place within the covenant. Against that background we see that it is a metaphorical turn that expresses what God does by election, prophetic critique and never-failing promise of a justice beyond imagination. Asking for forgiveness, submitting to judgement, looking to gift, hoping in a God-gifted future, allowing Christ to break down barriers, some peace may be restored, something of the fullness of the All Holy. The Church, sacramental presence of God's Christ and Spirit in a world weary of sin and death, lives by gift and always by gift and the central locus in its life for expressing this faith is where it keeps memorial of the self-annihilation of Christ who made himself sin. In the outpouring of the Spirit to those who are justified in Christ the Church learns to live by hope, a hope that is graceful in its eschatological expectation of the reign of this Father who so mercifully gives his Son and his Spirit. As 2 Peter 3.13–14 puts it, what is awaited is the place where righteousness, God's righteousness, will be at home.

Of living metaphors for a living body

Given the inherent dynamic and tension within scriptural language, we may appreciate that sacramental worship cannot be reduced to any rigidly controlled imagery or conceptualization. The act of sacramental worship in its remembrance must involve a remembering which is a listening, a heeding, a future-oriented recasting of the event that keeps its life precisely through this, even as we face into death and the death of meaning. Do not images, metaphors and the disturbances of time by scriptural proclamation have the energy to evoke imaginative ritual and remembrance in other times, places, cultures, historical settings? We live out the story as it has been passed on to us, relating back to its inner dynamic and tension. Sacrament as a gathering of assembly to remember and celebrate, means that we live out this story in new contexts and indeed adding as it were to the ongoing dynamic in a necessarily pluriform way. While the advent proclaimed in Christ of God's Word and Spirit is always the referent, and the eucharistic promise of gift always a hope and a hope for deliverance from judgement, we do not expect our issues and our questions to be answered or even considered in the scriptural texts themselves. But imaginative remembering drawing power out of the texts keeps on giving us a divine way of engaging with time, place and history. The times invite some change in the evocation of metaphors so that they may be saved from death to become anew living metaphors. Symbol and ritual systems solidify and over-determine signification and meaning. We cannot retrieve living poetics without passing through the death of meaning. This does not mean anything abrupt or tragic, though it is somewhat comic, since it requires that we see the incongruous in our ways of holding on to the Christ we think we know or the God we want. It is not entirely new in Christian times for believers to pass through such a death to find life. Indeed in the very origins of the Christian language of justification we witness Paul's need to die to standard meaning in discovering the truth of justification by faith, even while never forgetting the promises made in Abraham and in the Torah. Through the drama of the freedom of the Spirit, we have today another setting in which the story is to be remembered and to be led to contemplation by the prayer of doxology. The horizon is eschatological, which also means the place on which we stand is unsettled by the waves and the winds blowing us about in odd directions. There is to be a final judgement, when we come to know who and what Christ truly is, for now he is always becoming in his Body. At that moment, we hope to see the difference between good and evil, between life and death, when the gathered reality forged by human memories will either live for ever or enter death, simply 'die out'.

Body of Christ

To retrieve the narrative and metaphoric basis to sacramental memorial we need to think further about the presence of Christ and Spirit in the Church. There is a rich doctrine of the Spirit in Luther and Calvin, associated with Baptism and the Lord's Supper, but neither took this into liturgy nor sufficiently retrieved Augustine's sacramental grasp of the reality of Christ's Body through communion with him in the Spirit, so that there is but one Christ. The major contribution they made to a theology of the Church was to relocate Christ's presence, as it were. In recalling Christ's sacrifice, they stuck with the medieval paradigm of making satisfaction, but they located the saving faith in a different place, in the experience of sin and faith in Christ, in the hearing of the Word and the pledge of the Sacrament. In Augustinian terms it is through the 'four earthly sacraments' that Christ and Church are One Body, in the charity of the Spirit. What Graham Ward[9] brings out much more recently is that this Body is being constantly brought to completion within distinct historical and cultural settings and that only the action of the Spirit that looks back and looks forward can account for this. Christ takes form anew in those with whom he joins himself in word, faith and sacrament and will continue to do so until the end of time. It is in the power of the Spirit that the one Body of Christ takes on flesh in all the diversity and particularities of human reality. Though sacramental action is the memorial of *the ephapax* of Christ's Pasch, it is a becoming of the one Body of Christ in the particularities which it brings to expression through elements, rites and words.

The poet and artist David Jones[10] describes the act of Jesus at the Supper as a work of art, a blessing and a gesture of giving as 'a re-presentation' of all that is endured and bespoken in the anxiety of the Supper and in the betrayal unto death of the Friday. The gesture and the word are there to continue to present artistically this self-gift and to allow it to be given to all who in remembrance eat and drink. He is emphatic on the universality of Jesus' death given expression through the art of his supper action. When Christians celebrate this, it is not in some moment that transcends time but within the timeboundedness of those who live by this truth and this gift. As portrayed in the poem *In Parenthesis*,[11] Christ gives himself to soldiers in war and clothes himself in the mundane realities of the anxious soldiers, and all their own memories of life and family and friends. They live out this truth, without any claims to being heroic but just by living as they have to live day by day. The gift of Christ is received and lived out in those who commune with him, as they are given their place in time, in history, in a look, perhaps bleak, towards the future, but not letting memory die and so holding on to hope. Jones sees in Christ's death and its supper 're-presentation' an embrace of all that is human as he embodies some constant mythic and ritual patterns, recurring in a variety of cultures. We might today be less sure of the universal and more sensitive to the particular of culture, hoping that it is in the particular that Word and Spirit bring to us the Father's mercy and election. Accentuating the role of the poetic word allows for the diverse ways of pressing against reality, letting a long tradition of word and ritual give birth to fresh rather than simply repetitive expression. As said above, the words are associated with rites. Sharing food and drink from elemental things of the earth, as indeed looking to water and oil for sustenance and refreshment, conjures up the totality of peoples' dwelling on earth. It is through these that humans are gathered into nature's rhythms, as well as subjected to its, at times, devastating action. Plenty, sufficiency and famine, in their shaping of human existence, are all evoked, and it is in all of these moods and modes that the Body of Christ is shaped through the Spirit. When people are at one and in peace, the shared table, shared from the most fundamental resources of earth, gives expression to this harmony. When

people are divided, at odds, at war, experiencing injustice rather
then justice, the pain and efforts to be and live together are
expressed, perhaps only in a morsel, a crust, a deprivation. What
word can give sound and sight to this truth? Given limits of space
allotted, it is not possible to elaborate here on the residual power
of the images of kingdom, sacrifice and judgement. Attention is
given instead to another image that has had a strong impact on
contemporary theology. This is the image of *kenosis,* already
indeed employed as key in the Anaphora of Basil and in the
Roman Holy Week Liturgies. It may be able to capture our need
to look to Christ out of our weakness, seeing in him, in his
abasement, in his cross, the foolish weakness of the divine
Trinity. In his own ending he chose to make nothing of himself
in death and descent into hell. In sacrament there is the emptying out whereby he risks taking body in those who come to the
table, who are his Body here and now, and in hope for all time.
Christ is remembered in his drinking of death even unto the
dregs. He belongs among the most desolate of victims. His cru-
cifixion is not even remarkable: it is the lot meted out to many
accused of brigandry by the Roman soldiery. He is the victim of
betrayal and the failure of love. He has no power except that
which is from above, and so one that lives by the blessings of the
Sermon on the Mount, and only by these. This is the grace of
love; this is the act by which God justifies us. This is what takes
form, finds its time and place, through the life of the Body by
which Christ takes on shape and visibility across ages. Some
author may find it possible through this image to write a memorial prayer that is a contemporary poetics of justification. To pray
well in our time, there is much death to meaning to pass through,
much ecclesial self-emptying in communion with Christ's, but
it is in the art of praying *de profundis* that we know that God is
with us, raising us up, in the gift of his word and Spirit. In the
end, sacramentality resides in the complex memorial action
which allows us to see how the love of God given in Christ and
Spirit has been poured out into weak humans, in their use of the
powerfully weak things of earth. This love resides in God's gift
given through the human encounter with the totality of the

human, and with the realities of earth, sky, gods and mortals that is embodied in both the plenty and the want of bread, wine, oil and water, of each place and people. If in the midst of life's weakness some find other signs of such a grace, it may be asked how they partake of the generous love of God thus shown.

Notes

1 See Peter Bouteneff and Dagmar Heller (eds), *Interpreting Together: Essays in Hermeneutics* (Geneva: WCC Publications, Faith and Order Paper no. 189, 2001).

2 This heuristic is presented in this author's book, *Sacrament: The Language of God's Giving* (New York: Crossroad, 1999), esp. pp. 74–95.

3 See Seamus Heaney, *Crediting Poetry: The Nobel Lecture* (New York: Farrar, Straus & Giroux, 1995).

4 For practical purposes, one may consult the English translations in R. C. D. Jasper and G. J. Cuming, *Prayers of the Eucharist: Early and Reformed* (New York: Pueblo Publishing Company, 1987. Reprinted by The Liturgical Press as a Pueblo Book).

5 Ulrich S. Leopold (ed.), 'Liturgy and Hymns', *Luther's Works*, vol. 53 (Philadelphia: Fortress Press, 1965), pp. 256–7.

6 *Together in Mission and Ministry: the Porvoo Statement, with Essays on Church and Ministry in Northern Europe* (London: Church House Publishing 1993), Part III, 32 c.

7 For more, see Jason J. Ripley, 'Covenantal Concepts of Justice and Righteousness, and Catholic-Protestant Reconciliation: Theological Interpretations and Explorations', *Journal of Ecumenical Studies* 38 (Winter 2001), pp. 95–108.

8 See the many meanings offered in even a small work, *A Concise Greek-English Dictionary of the New Testament*, prepared by Barclay M. Newman, Jr (Stuttgart: Deutsche Bibelgesellschaft, 1993), p. 46.

9 Graham Ward, 'Bodies: The Displaced Body of Jesus Christ', in John Milbank, Catherine Pickstock and Graham Ward (eds), *Radical Orthodoxy* (London & New York: Routledge, 1999), pp. 163–81.

10 David Michael Jones, 'Art and Sacrament', in Harman Grisewood (ed.), *Epoch and Artist: Selected Writings* (London: Faber, 1959), pp. 147ff.
11 David M. Jones, *In Parenthesis* (London: Faber, 1937; pbk edition 1963).

10

Finding new sense in the 'sacramental'

Ann Loades

My concern is to rediscover a way of thinking, imagining 'Christianly' something of the character of God's relation to the world (whatever there is), a way which we neglect, and that to our cost. I assume the following convictions to be fundamental. First, to say the obvious about the 'world': the context in which we find ourselves is not 'ours', because it belongs to, and is derived from, another. Human discovery and rediscovery of this world by whatever means is an inexhaustible source of wonder and gratitude. Ours is a world of astonishingly rich texture and complexity, of bodiliness and flesh, exhibiting divine largesse, certainly, but often deeply problematic. Second, I presuppose theological realism, or in other words, 'God' as other than us, not available for our possession or control, ultimately unnameable, unsayable, unsafe in the sense of being utterly free and finally unpredictable, and beyond our idolatries (including what we take to be 'real' even of God in godself). God lies beyond our self-intoxication, self-preoccupation, delusions, needs and harms, but does not leave human beings to flounder in their pains and difficulties but seeks them out, summons them beyond what will stunt and atrophy them to become fully normal human persons – saints. In that sense at least God is necessary. Third, God's invitation to human beings is that they be caught up with all other creatures into the exchange of love and generosity at the heart of the divine, into the exuberance of the whole 'company of heaven', sharing the conviviality and the companionship of a re-possessed paradise, encompassing more than we can presently imagine. Fourth, the specifically Christian conviction is that this invitation is from the God who not merely flesh-makes but flesh-takes, in some measure becoming sayable in his seeking, and it is God alone who continues to initiate such mediation of divine presence as may be possible to us and for us. Fifth, the key inter-pretative category here is 'sacramentality', which as Archbishop Rowan Williams reminds us in his Foreword to this volume, is not a general principle that the world is full of 'sacredness'. Rather, 'it is the very specific conviction that the world is full of the life of a God whose nature is known in Christ and the Spirit'. We remind ourselves that it is primarily in worship that we invoke 'God, Christ, Spirit', and that central to Christian worship is a meal (of a kind) which insistently reminds us that the divine seeking of human persons is redemptive – we cannot be left as we are, and we cannot extricate ourselves from our pre-dicaments solely by our own efforts, though we might by God's grace be enabled to do what we must and can. Redemption, above all, requires the creativity of God, and it is crucial to keep this in mind when rediscovering 'sacramentality'. I shall return later to this emphasis.

In consideration of 'sacramentality' as the divine initiative to mediate divine redemptive presence to us, we need to be alert to the dangers closely associated with it. We cannot 'cause' that presence, least of all in the most authoritative, symbolically complex form we can devise in liturgy. A human self-making of divine presence is a contradiction in terms and a thoroughly futile endeavour. To speak of the mediation of divine presence, transfiguring or blessing or gracing our world or some part or aspect of it, has everything to do with simply allowing for the possibility of it, of relishing it wherever it just so happens to be around, to surface perhaps, to be not merely unmistakably but perhaps even very ambiguously just 'there'. Further, divine presence may very properly be associated with the fleeting, the contingent, here today and gone tomorrow, with 'travelling light'. Indeed, most of the 'material signs' of specific sacraments or of sacramental practices are fluid, or consumable, transient, except in their immediate or longer term effects on human persons. We may think here of bread, wine, oil, ashes, water, candle flames, hands in blessing, words in preaching and praying, making the sign of the cross, standing, processing, kneeling and genuflecting, singing, exchanging 'peace', making a confession of faith, saying the Lord's prayer, reading and performing texts of the liturgy, reading Scripture, participating by listening to the singing of a choir, contributing to charitable collections gener-ously, pleading for mercy. Liturgy requires preparation, thought, care and full attention, but it has much to do with the tempo-rary and the 'throw-away', and this emphasis could be of great importance in societies transfixed by obsessions about recording everything, with analysis, dissection and the 'countable'. It is at least arguable that in such societies we need to de-stabilize the sense that only these things are real. What is real cannot be reduced to what can be frozen or fixed for our attention, or reconstructed to suit our interests, but consistently avoids our grasp and greed. We tread very warily in reflecting on the sacra-mental, therefore, avoiding on the one hand attributing to persons and to things power or powers they do not, should not, or cannot have, and on the other, supposing that the things we find around us, or that we make, or our very own persons, are so problematic that we find ourselves thoroughly at odds with our divinely given context. We may not always be able to distin-guish easily between nausea and disgust at ourselves as appropri-ate responses to our self-wrought harms, hideous as some of them are, and disgust at the world in which we find ourselves. That disgust may have its part to play in recognizing the world as sacramental but it cannot be the most appropriate 'mood' for appreciating the world as God-derived and blessed. On the other hand, if the horror and squalor of a judicial execution can mediate God to us, so in principle might what we take at first sight to be the banal, the squalid, even the morally problematic. We will need all the resources of knowledge, imagination, emotion and understanding we can find, from whatever source, exercised with discrimination and sensitivity to be alert to divine presence, and no one is uniquely privileged here. Catholicity requires not simply attention to the whole, but drawing on the resources of the whole. That 'whole' includes all that 'tradition' can offer us in its splendid and disturbing complexity. It is my view, in other words, that it is of crucial importance for the rediscovery of the sacramental that we have a sense not only of the present but of the past that is both handed on to us and to which and for which we are responsible in our turn. We have only to look at what happens to any human group when a stronger group systematically destroys their past as part of a strategy for destroying them. Tradition is not to be construed as 'the dead hand of the past' which will prevent us from thinking afresh, but a life-giving source of vitality, and just how human beings live with one another and with all else is fascinating, even if we look no further than Christianity itself. We might look, for instance, at the lives of the saints who feast with Christ in his generosity, including the almost 'nobodies', the barely remembered who may nonetheless have shown utter fidelity to God in the courage of their living and dying. They represent an astonishing range of imaginative possibilities, and for and in our time it is of great importance that at last the bodily presence of the 'Eves' of the world are recollected and reflected upon, in and of themselves, not as mimetic 'males', as one mark of a renewed sacramentality. Tradition should be seen as of its essence creative and innovative, mustering every grace of intelligence and skill in enabling us to learn from the past, generate critical dissonance with the present, open up new vistas and walkways, generate new insights, negotiate dead ends, endure experiences of profound alienation, and live with criteria which themselves may change, or if they remain more or less constant, will change in their application. In the re-discovery of the sacramental, therefore, the past as past does not and should not control the present or the future, and at one level we are all perfectly familiar with this. If we were not, we would not be able to say the Apostles' Creed, let alone the Nicene (both of them 'sacramental'), at the appropriate points in our liturgies. In the case of the former creed, attention to what can be known about its history reveals the introduction of novel clauses into the earlier ground-creeds so far as we can discover them, and a long and fascinating history of interpretation of those clauses in varying social and political contexts, which indeed continues. In the case of the Nicene Creed, its theologically innovative language and commitments reveal a notably contentious history. Taking a clue from Rowan Williams' conviction that 'the world is full of the life of a God whose nature is known in Christ and the Spirit', we might even suggest that another mark of the renewal of the sacramental would be found in the traditionalists as 'spirit-bearers', or say of them that they are 'pneumatophoric', to use a word from Orthodoxy. One could hardly make the claim to be 'pneu-matophoric' for oneself, nor limit it to particular office-holders – it would be attributed to some persons by others, and to those persons-with-others. Another way of putting this could be to say that some persons are 'graced presences' for others, for 'grace' has an unmistakably 'bodily' resonance. To say 'that was a graceful gesture' is not simply to make a remark about how someone moves (though Canova's statue of the three eminently feminine 'Graces' reminds us of the physical beauty of grace), but it is indissolubly associated with movement of some kind. So we might well think of sacramentality in terms of 'inner conviction of visible or experienceable grace or graces', evident in lively and committed tradition-bearers, capable of the innovative creativ-ity which gives us some inkling of what creativity is in God, and I suggest that it is in many forms of creativity that human beings discern sacramentality, and that in a diversity of ways.

Human beings turn readily to the 'natural' world, the context in which they find themselves, for a sense of divine presence, which they may well associate with the unviolated, the unspoiled, though what appears to be 'natural' is at least some-times or to some extent a matter of creative contrivance, as, for instance, in the provision of clean water or the presentation of a landscape, or the ways in which we learn to look at landscape. If not to the natural, human creatures turn to the specific realm of human making, of *poiesis*. Poetry, the word, the peculiarly human resources of metaphorical language in all its dimensions, is undeniably important in the purely gratuitous mediation of the sense of divine presence. Word, made flesh, may indeed be full of grace and truth, making known to us what we need to know and to love, even for instance in the nightmare betrayal of the trust and hospitality shown to a most honoured friend and guest in John 13. Perhaps initially we may be inclined to think of the importance of 'word' in relation to prayers, to hymns and to preaching – to which I shall return. There are, however, other means of mediation by 'word' as in drama, and in many other forms of communication, more or less or only tangentially verbal.

Thus music has its own infinitely extensive 'vocabulary' quite apart from its particular alliances with human voices, and it is embodied, with or without the instruments which become 'body' for the performer on them. Cinema, film and photography, advertising, may or may not be explicitly verbal, as may dance – and that not only in 'musicals'. And we certainly can and must talk about glass-making, gardening, engineering, design, fashion and clothing, sculpture, metalwork, embroidering, food, buildings, public space and the use we make of it. For many human beings, even if they are not themselves 'genetic' parents, being involved with the very young will require ingenuity and creativity to a remarkable degree. Also for many, the worlds of work, paid or not, private or public, and our manifold forms of creativity which come to expression in social and political life need to be seen as sacramental, not least when we have identified the importance of the flair and problem-solving skills of the manager and the entrepreneur and the 'fixer'. Just as narrowly construed religious perspective may miss what Karl Rahner referred to as the divine depth of ordinary life, it may also miss the importance of the public, shared world. Sacramentality may require a certain sort of willingness to live somewhat on the edge of danger and difficulty, with something of the invigorating panache and cheerfulness found in the world of the entrepreneurs. No doubt we need to recover certain ways of patterning life by sacramental practices, and of developing certain strengths (virtues) associated with that patterning – faith, fortitude, charity, justice, prudence, temperance and hope, but we may need not just these to add to the biblical lists of fruits of the spirit, but new ways of thinking and living about the gifts needed. These, as yet to be discerned, will enable us to live sacramentally in our risky, mistake-ridden, very complex world. Nothing less will be needed to sustain the praise of God for the splendours of creation and redemption even in the most appalling circumstances, not least the praise sacramentally sustained in liturgy.

My view is that it is in liturgy that we learn and are lured to God in certain very specific ways, so that if liturgy is bungled, the consequences are very serious, and its consideration is far too important to be left to the periphery of theology, or to training for ordination. Nor is liturgy reducible to learning about rubrics, or to who wears what and why, to how things were done or what was said in the remote past, important though such elements of tradition may be, or to how many sacraments there are, or might be. All of these have some degree of importance, in connection with the fundamental point that it is in the course of engagement with a certain kind of ceremonious activity that we are enabled to say 'God', and having learned to say 'God' may be able to discern God beyond the framework of liturgy, as I have just suggested. So, however simple the liturgy, however pared down, whatever the balance of the verbal or non-verbal (and giving the highest importance to preaching as sacramental) it is because we do this or that, sing these hymns, or not, repeat these words, and so on, that we begin to find sense in doctrine. Actions have to be clothed with the right words, and once the right words have been found, these, in their turn, have to be 'performed' by particular speakers or singers with certain authoritative roles in communion with others. We need to recover the sense of obligation to be present at liturgy, which is *not* reducible to the Eucharist, and to see attendance at it as analogous to the necessity of yeast for bread and salt for food. Rediscovering the sacramental must find its specifically Christian source here, whilst not resting there, but it takes time, as do many other serious forms of human activity. Anyone who has seriously engaged in learning a skill – from learning to walk and learning to speak as a child – knows the importance of repetition, and in this case it is the learning of praise, of expressions of gratitude, of petition, the practise of stillness and silence, the maturity of confession and repentance, and the sense of words such as grace and glory, body, blood, water and fire, bread, wine, death, resurrection and ascension, divine judgement, re-creation. All these take time to learn, and we cannot underestimate the difficulty of convincing people that they must be there, or of sustaining their commitment to one another by their very presence. In societies where for a time it seems difficult for people to commit themselves to any institution, this may initially seem to be an intractable problem, but it must be attempted. Without it, the sacramental may escape us.

Since, as we know, liturgy is essentially 'public service', undertaken by the Church for the sake of the world, it is then incumbent on all the baptized to take to themselves the responsibility by the living of doctrine to make the common holy, and make the holy common – another way of referring to the rediscovery of the sense of the sacramental. There will also need to be a certain sense of 'being in training', if the senses and appetites of human beings are not to be surfeited and sated so that capacity for the sacramental is as it were suffocated in us. We need to discern together what we need to give up in order to be freed up to gain the life that matters, and resist every pressure to assess who we are in terms of what we have, which can so easily seep into every aspect of even our most private selves. We need to be able to say 'No' as a mark of maturity, and we need shared practices such as those of Lent or other penitential seasons so to learn it, being able to delight in gifts of redemption when they are on offer to us. Isak Dinesen/Karen Blixen's short story of 'Babette's Feast' (in her collection *Anecdotes of Destiny*) is a brilliant example of one experience of redemption, brought in the very person of the cook, Babette, herself a refugee from terror. We also need to renegotiate certain dichotomies which have come to mark Christian communities off in contradistinction from one another: being fallen/being sanctified; justification/holiness; word and obedience/sacrament and participation, and so on. All this may require our actual physical presence at one another's liturgies, however excluded or unwelcome we may feel at least at first, as we experience unfamiliar ways of opening human beings up to God. Particularly we need to explore the multiplicity of meanings of Baptism and Eucharist, and their transformation of those most elementary acts of washing and feeding without which no child can survive; and the connections of both with penitence and forgiveness without which we cannot go on. We need the richness of difference to sustain people in their very different circumstances, but not to play these out in such a way that they divide us from one another.

I turn briefly now to one element of liturgy which is too easily overlooked in thinking about the sense of the sacramental, and that is preaching. A thoroughly sacramental sensitivity will, I suggest, also give pride of place to preaching, precisely because of its sheer variability, echoing something of the complexity of Scripture, tradition, varied experience and thoughtful reflection upon all these. There is no one understanding of how divine Word and human word are related in preaching, whether, for instance, the preacher mediates the self-giving of God, or heralds and witnesses to that self-giving as it seizes the imaginations and understandings of the hearers so that they may make decisions they might not otherwise have made, particularly that of conversion to God. The preacher may fundamentally challenge our whole understanding of our lives; evoke courage and hope and the awareness of God's presence in even the most shattered community or particular life. Preachers need also to listen to those who hear them in specific liturgical settings, so that their own understandings are renewed by the graced responses of their communities, however inchoate and incoherent some of those responses may be. We might especially thankfully acknowledge as sacramental particular moments when hitherto unsuspected possibilities open up – creative discontinuities stirred into life by the catalyst of a preacher's words – words themselves having become part of the network of grace. So a holistic sacramental theology might see that preaching, however understood, is never dispensable. Human beings learn in many ways, but much depends upon being taught, and there are more ways of teaching than simply saying something, but it must be among the responsibilities of a preacher to initiate and sustain response to God's generosity, looking both for what we might call sacramental continuities in practices we can identify – stemming from attendance at liturgy – and for the sacramental discontinuities of unsuspected opportunity. Both of these manifestations of sacramental redemption deserve some moments of reflection, as in the following paragraphs.

There are well tried modes of response to divine generosity which need constantly to be taught, and never taken for granted, such as 'corporal' and 'spiritual' works of mercy. The former are those which may rightly be associated with Isaiah 58.6–9, the great parable of Matthew 25.31–46 and with Tobit 1–2, the provision of bodily mercies of food and drink to the needy, clothing and shelter to the destitute, visits to the sick and imprisoned, and the provision of burial for the dead, any or all of which may require much sensitivity and creativity. 'Spiritual' works of mercy are to convert the sinner, to instruct the ignorant, counsel the doubtful, comfort the sorrowful, learn to bear wrongs patiently, pray for the living and the faithful (and unfaithful) departed, and forgive injuries. Whether formalized as 'works of mercy' or not, these priorities need to be identified and practised, but if we need to emphasize any one responsibility of the preacher at the present time, we might focus especially on the need to foster the 'creative discontinuity' of forgiveness, opening up the future so that we are neither defined by the undoubted wrongs we do or the wrong done to us. Human beings need at least release from what they have done unknowingly, but for forgiveness to be possible, they also need the language of lament (such as Psalm 130), both for their own malice and capacity to harm, and to find the determination to refuse and overcome the wrongs done to them by others, or the wrongs they have themselves committed, in so far as that is humanly possible. Some things may have to be thought of as safely left to God, not least if we are to avoid the

kind of sinfulness which supposes that justice is only appropriately expressed in retribution, rather than in continued prayer for
the sanctification of the 'enemy' and the descents into hell which
human beings bring upon one another. Such prayer is integral
to lament, which needs to be seen to be sacramental, keeping
human beings in touch with that sense of justice itself which
manifests divine presence, notwithstanding so many difficulties
in establishing where justice may lie. We have also to endure
some measure of ignorance about what justice may require, and
thus what forgiveness may mean in all circumstances. We more
certainly can identify moments when forgiveness may be prema-
turely requested, and see that 'letting-go' may only be possible at
the end of a long process of remembering, recalling, giving up
denial, enduring the pain of recovered feeling, sharing anger,
and receiving much blessing of the body in sacramental acts of
healing and anointing and whatever other means of comfort may
be available to help someone recover a God-given sense of self-
worth. Whether or not it becomes possible to pray for one's
'enemy' would be a further step along that road, but at least in
the Christian dispensation not everybody has to do everything:
excruciatingly difficult tasks such as this one may have to be left
to others in the 'body'. One mark of recovery might be the discovery of a sense of humour, however grim or ironic, another
largely neglected sacramental in theology, and certainly in
liturgy, yet a central resource for the human comedy, as so many
cultures display, and which Christian traditions so largely ignore.

In conclusion, I turn briefly from what may at first glance be
thought to be the realm of the personal understood as private,
to the realm of the public, in which forgiveness too has its
undoubted place. For we need to rediscover that God is also to
be found in the life of the city, as paradoxically the creeds, the
Kyrie and the *Sanctus* may indicate. In these we declare loyalty to
and dependence upon God, and put even the best of the 'lords'
of this world in their places. Therefore, as part of the 'public
service' which should flow from liturgy which insistently orien-
tates human beings towards God, we may be enabled again to
pitch in to the negotiation of 'common' good in institutions of

many kinds. Much discussion of sacramentality avoids even beginning to grapple with the 'graces' of institutional and political life. Sacramentality is not, fundamentally, a utilitarian concept, that is to say, it is not primarily concerned with its 'usefulness' to us, but we may permit ourselves to think that it may indeed be found to be useful in so far as its rediscovery may transform us in our dealings with one another in many walks of life. We might learn to grace one another through life, as God graces us, not least by learning the habits of intradependence: 'Abide in me as I in you'. Certainly of crucial importance in political and institutional life would be the re-learning of habits of hope, trust and covenant, well beyond the boundaries of the conventionally 'religious' or sacramental. These remarks conclude my present reflections on the importance of the sense of the sacramental, and much remains to be explored in detail of my ambitious proposals. I hope that it is obvious, however, that I am unambiguously committed to its importance – and that well beyond predictable boundaries.

11

Music, mystery and sacrament

Jeremy S. Begbie

What can be gained from describing music as sacramental? Given music's ability to grasp and overwhelm us in ways which elude words, the mediation of this experience through physical materials, and the pervasiveness of music in the religions of the world (including Christianity), it would not be surprising if we found ourselves wanting to use sacramental language of music. And in due course I want to suggest that there are legitimate and fruitful ways of doing so. However, the fact that virtually no contemporary theologians have chosen to do so should at least give us pause for thought. There are, I believe, good reasons for being quite cautious about making the music–sacrament link too hastily. I shall begin this essay by attempting to throw some of them into relief, in conversation with what is by far the most sustained attempt in recent times to speak of music sacramentally, Albert Blackwell's *The Sacred in Music*.[1]

The sacred in music

Blackwell draws on a broad range of sources (as diverse as Augustine, Calvin, Jonathan Edwards, Schleiermacher, Tillich and Weil) to demonstrate what he calls the 'sacramental potential' of music. He concentrates on wordless, instrumental music and understands 'sacramental' as applying to 'any finite reality through which the divine is perceived to be disclosed and communicated, and through which our human response to the divine assumes some measure of shape, form, and structure'.[2] Music has sacramental potency at its heart, Blackwell contends, awaiting times and places for its actualization. Expanding on this, Blackwell delineates two broad traditions of sacramental encounter in Christianity which have been applied to music: the 'Pythagorean' and the 'incarnational'. In the first, stretching through Plato, Boethius, Augustine and much medieval thought, music enables the intellectual apprehension of the world's mathematical harmony, the ratios and proportions which configure created reality. And this can lead – in at least some versions of the theory – to the apprehension of God's beauty and harmony.[3] Blackwell appropriates this tradition in a particular manner. He points to the way in which 'the fundaments of music are grounded in acoustical realities, given and enduring' in the physical world, transcending culture and historical particularity.[4] He makes much of the phenomenon of the 'harmonic series'. A string in a piano vibrates not only across its whole length but also in halves, thirds, quarters and so on, these extra vibrations creating a series of 'overtones' or 'harmonics' which sound along with the lowest tone. Blackwell shows how musical strategies from a vast range of cultures are rooted in this phenomenon.[5] He concedes that the harmonic series can be engaged and developed in very different ways, but insists that, at least to some extent, all music negotiates this 'given' of nature. Reflection on this, he believes, can open up the possibility of 'a sense of trust in cosmic order' which in turn can lead to 'trust in the second Person of the Trinity', the *Logos* of the world. In short, music exhibits created rationalities which can be read as divine 'signatures' and can thus lay the intellectual ground for subsequent faith in the Author of these rationalities.[6] If the 'Pythagorean' tradition stresses the intellectual apprehension of the imperceptible, the 'incarnational' stresses the sensed materiality of music, the latter tradition being an 'essential counterpoise' to the former, hingeing as it does on construing music as a thoroughly sensual, bodily experience. Drawing loosely on Schleiermacher and others, Blackwell links embodied musical perception to a primordial religious awareness of the ultimate givenness of our lives and the world, of being wholly dependent on and immersed in a limitless ground. This is epitomized in 'oceanic' musical experiences: in listening to the second movement of Brahms' fourth symphony, for example, Blackwell writes of having had 'an engulfing sense of indissoluble bond, of intimacy with the overpowering vastness of the world'.[7] Aware that his double-stranded vision might neglect the world's tragedy, in a series of extended reflections on the Fall, Blackwell contends that music is not only caught up in the ambiguities of sin and evil but has distinctive resources to express life's 'terrible beauty': tonal tension, harmonic dissonance, acoustical interference, and minor modes.[8] Turning to music's redemptive possibilities, he maintains that music 'can help to save a fallen world',[9] as a gift not only of God's general grace (an outgrowth of natural acoustics) and special grace (a medium of human creativity), but also of saving grace (a vehicle of healing and harmony).[10] Concluding the book, Blackwell speaks of music's power to outstrip language, and correlates this with a variety of Christian mystical experiences, encounters with a transcendence infinitely greater than ourselves.

Misgivings

With limited space, I have only been able to indicate the shape of Blackwell's argument and highlight some of its key features. Undoubtedly, we are offered a deeply attractive and generous vision, bolstered by highly persuasive musical analyses (he includes some particularly telling critiques of postmodern analytical fashions). Nevertheless, I want to register some misgivings, both theological and musicological. The first concerns a tendency to use sacramental language in such a way that *the freedom and distinctiveness of the created world in relation to God is weakened*. Blackwell is keen to ground music's order in the created world at large, and through that, in God's own eternity – this is part of a 'panentheistic' vision that would celebrate a truly cosmic presence of the divine. While being very sympathetic to the rooting of music in creation at large, and affirming God's presence in and to the world, we might ask: does not his eagerness to correlate musical order and God's eternity need to be balanced by a somewhat stronger stress on the world's distinctiveness? It is one thing to speak of the orderliness of the acoustic world as enduring, reliable, permanent and given (and as such testifying to God's faithfulness). It is quite another to flirt with the notion – as Blackwell seems to do in at least one place – that acoustic laws are 'moving images of eternity',[11] especially when history shows that many 'laws' turn out not to be laws, or at least laws of a rather different kind than might initially be supposed. There are few better illustrations of the dangers here than the waning of the very Pythagorean vision Blackwell so admires. From the sixteenth century it was shown that the order of sound did not quite match up to the ancient mathematics supposedly underwritten by God, and this precipitated (needless) theological crises. It is regrettable that in music theory this contributed to a marked distancing of music from God-given cosmic order, and indeed from God.[12] Arguably, what is required here is a robust recognition of the created world as possessing its own particular order – an order that is upheld and permeated by the Creator's activity, but nonetheless one which is to be discovered and elicited in its otherness and distinctiveness. 'Graced' by God the world may be, but the grace of the triune God of Jesus Christ entails a respect of, and commitment to, the other *as other*.[13] The other side of this concerns the freedom of God – and this is my second unease: the tendency for sacramental language to be used in such a way that *God's free and purposeful agency is muffled*. The logical form of the book's thesis seems to run thus: 'musical sounds mediate (or can mediate) divine presence'. The advantage of construing the sacramental dynamic this way is that it encourages us to take the material properties of the medium seriously – in this case, musical sounds. The disadvantage is that it risks muting God's prevenient intentional activity, God's *movement toward* the world, especially if metaphors of presence are favoured over metaphors of action.[14] To be sure, Blackwell is not denying God's agency in music, nor claiming that music should usurp God's powers, or that God should be put at music's disposal. Nevertheless, that

God's interaction with the world might involve particular actions, bringing about states of affairs that are not merely a function of the world's own immanent possibilities, is a notion conspicuous by its absence. Indeed, little is said about the divine nature and character; what is asserted is largely by way of negation, at times leaving the impression – ironically – that music is rather more interesting than God. All this is of a piece with the relative absence of eschatological momentum. There is much about eschatological consummation, but little of the New Testament's sense that revelation in the present is (as much as anything else) a revelation of what *will be*, of the future breaking in through Christ and the Spirit, of a radical re-ordering of our history, made possible through the disruption of cross and resurrection, of the Gospel as enacted promise – and very little awareness that music might be singularly well equipped to embody just these dynamics. Significantly, far more is said about harmony than about rhythm and metre. If the word 'incarnational' is to be used to draw attention to music's materiality, the same must surely be said of its temporality (the Incarnation being both material and temporal) – music's ability to re-shape, re-configure our temporal co-ordinates.[15] A third unease: it is somewhat odd to find a theology of sacrament that appeals regularly to the Christian Scriptures but appears to *evade the kind of christological determination such an appeal would seem to require*. Blackwell's preference for the terms 'the sacred', or 'the divine' rather than 'God', signals a marked reluctance to specify and characterize this God as the God of Jesus Christ, and to follow through the methodological obligations of such a specification.[16] Here the impact of nineteenth-century idealism (and more recently Paul Tillich) is especially evident: the coming of Christ is interpreted as an instance of creation's general openness to ultimate reality, and the term 'incarnation' commandeered accordingly. A christological reading of creation, divine presence and encounter is exchanged for an ontology trawled from a range of sources, of which the narrative of Jesus Christ is but one.[17] My *theological* misgivings are intertwined with a third, a *musicological* unease. To focus this: there is a prevailing model of musical experience in Blackwell's argument which I think compounds some of his theological difficulties, as well as importing some new ones of its own. It is surprisingly common in Christian discussions about music. The model is of *a person sitting in silent stillness, listening in rapt aesthetic attention to the sounds of a great work*. A cluster of musical sounds constitutes an aesthetic 'object', in the presence of which a particular attitude is required, where we are to 'listen to' music 'for its own sake', refusing to use it for pre-determined purposes, and consider it apart from any social or cultural contexts or ends. The ideal experience is as far as possible one in which mediators (performers, scores, the body) are rendered transparent, for the sake of an experience of the immediacy of sounds. The invention of the concert hall answered to just this kind of model, and the associated genre became instrumental music, stripped of extra-musical references, allusions, and so forth ('absolute' music, epitomized in the untitled and wordless symphonies of Beethoven). Blackwell does speak of other models of musical experience, but this would seem to be the predominant one informing his account of music's potential sacramentality.[18] Undoubtedly, this model accounts for at least part of what is going on in the musical experience of millions, and some of the finest music ever produced has been written with just this kind of model in mind. However, difficulties arise if we treat it as a kind of normative paradigm, an ideal to which we should aspire. Three comments are in order here. (a) We should not miss the *strongly theological overtones* implicit in the model. Nicholas Wolterstorff writes: 'Anyone who, with open eyes, reads the writing about art from the last two centuries cannot help but be struck by the religiosity of it'. Around the notion of the autonomy of art, he continues, 'we have constructed an ideology in which such art is seen as transcending the alienation of everyday society. To immerse oneself in a work of art is to enter a higher realm – a realm of freedom and transcendent universality'.[19] Asking why such a view has developed in the modern West, he comments that 'part of the answer will have to take note of the fact that as the Christian religion lost its grip on the minds and hearts of western humanity, some filled the gap with faith in the present and future wonders of science and technology, while others filled it with Art'.[20] Those keen to speak of music as sacramental cannot afford to ignore the dangers to which Wolterstorff alludes, and the unthinking adoption of this particular aesthetic of musical perception as paradigmatic is unlikely to help. (b) Even as a description of musical experience, the model is severely lacking. Not only is it relatively recent and culturally localized, but when assumed to be exemplified (as in, say, a concert hall), it is inadequate, for *it tends to abstract musical sounds from their associated practices.* A growing number of music theorists urge that we should see the foundational realities of music not as works but as a set of *practices* (from which 'works' may or may not emerge), the most basic of these being *music-making and music-hearing.*[21] These practices are irreducibly bodily, social (involving relations between persons), and cultural (bound up with the patterns of thought and action characteristic of particular groups). Music is not so much an 'object' as a way of being in the world, a way of negotiating the realities we inhabit. Many will be understandably nervous about such a 'functionalist' approach to music; they will be concerned to preserve the integrity of musical sounds (including their aesthetic character). But a moment's thought shows that music is nonetheless always functional, always playing a role – and bringing aesthetic delight in a concert hall is one such. The range of roles is virtually limitless. Music can help put a baby to sleep, mobilize an army, symbolize national identity, provoke physical response, or demarcate social boundaries. A non-Western or non-European perspective quickly makes this apparent. The Exeter sociologist Tia DeNora opens her book, *Music in Everyday Life*, with a telling anecdote:

> On a drizzly Saturday morning in July 1998, I was sheltering under a tree in a North London market, conducting a series of impromptu interviews with women on the topic of 'music in their lives' . . . During a lull, the market manager wandered over to ask what I was doing. He told me he was originally from Nigeria, where, he said

with emphasis, they 'really knew' how to use music. The situation was different in the United Kingdom, he said, where people did not seem to be aware of music's powers, and did not respect its social and physiological force. As he saw it, Europeans merely *listened* to music, whereas in Africa people *made* music as an integral element of social life.[22]

We might want to nuance that by speaking of making *and hearing* music, and, of course, there are many different forms of African music – but the main point still holds. To ask about 'the sacramental potential' of music, then, is to ask about musical sounds, certainly, but as made and heard by flesh-and-blood people in complex, concrete, intentional contexts. Significantly, this is in line with much recent writing on sacrament which has stressed the embeddedness of sacramental materials in corporate action, in social and cultural matrices. (c) The model attempts *to abstract musical sounds not only from practices but from other modes of perceiving and negotiating the world.* It is bewitched by the myth of 'music alone', that we receive musical sounds 'neat'. But a seventeen-year old hears a rock group *along with* images on a giant screen; we hear Dido *while* scanning a range of shirts in Gap; even in a concert hall, we hear Beethoven's seventh symphony *along with* seeing the gestures of an energetic conductor, the quasi-dance of the timpanist, and so on. 'Music alone' is an aesthetician's fiction. Indeed, just because music is weak at referring to extra-musical phenomena with any consistency and precision, it makes particularly close associations with other media, especially human words.[23] This is not to downplay the particular capacities of musical sounds, but if we are to explore music's 'sacramental potential' we need to treat these interactions as integral to musical experience. To pull this together: our uneasiness about bringing music and the language of the 'sacramental' together is that we will too easily be constrained by theologically questionable assumptions about material entities mediating divine reality, and/or by a limited and potentially distorting account of musical experience, and – when they occur together – by their mutual reinforcement.

Another way of hearing things?

Might there be other ways in which sacramental language might be better appropriated for music – and indeed, enriched *by* music – ways which take into account the hazards we have noted? I can do no more here than chart a direction by examining one piece in one tradition, the opening chorus of J. S. Bach's *St Matthew Passion* – '*Kommt, ihr Töchter*'. We shall limit ourselves to considering the piece largely in its original context, without denying the possibility that much of what applied to the piece's sacramental capacity in Bach's day could apply today,[24] and we shall concentrate largely on the particular contribution of the musical sounds to this capacity. This mammoth fantasia lifts the curtain on almost three hours of musical drama. It was designed for the church of St Thomas in Leipzig, where Bach worked from 1723 to 1750, and was probably first heard there in 1727.[25] The sounds Bach devised, then, were conceived as interacting with a very particular building (with a two-and-a-half-second reverberation), particular patterns of seating, visibility and so on – together with a particular congregation, and particular singers and players. We cannot here examine the music's interactions with all these particularities, but we can at least consider the most basic contextual factor of all, namely its setting in corporate worship. The piece was written for the service of Vespers on Good Friday afternoon, a preaching service centred on a Bible reading and sermon. The *Passion* setting itself provided the biblical text (together with commentary on that text[26]), and the sermon would be delivered in between its two main parts.[27] Not only is the liturgical setting homiletic, there is every reason to suppose that the *Passion* itself was understood in the same way, as an integral part of its proclamatory dynamic.[28] The musical sounds were thought to aid the proclamation of the Passion story and enable the congregation to participate in its drama. Put more theologically, the aim was that through the Spirit they would not only hear the Gospel in and through the drama, but be able to appropriate its saving power for themselves, as they were drawn to the central figure, Jesus Christ.[29] This might well be described as 'contemplation' or 'meditation',[30] but it is not of the sort that is concerned chiefly with the pleasure afforded by patterns of musical sounds 'for their own sake', and certainly not of the sort where words become irrelevant, but where music's distinctive powers draw a congregation to share in the realities of which the words speak and in which the words are caught up. I have used the phrase 'music's distinctive powers' quite deliberately, for what I have just described may sound to many like word-fixated Protestant instrumentalism at its worst: when music becomes the slave of words, its unique properties rendered redundant in the eagerness to 'get the message across'. And, some will want to add, this linguistic infatuation is just what sacramental theology needs to shun today. But a closer look at this piece reveals something far subtler and immensely instructive for sacramental theology: *as music interacts with words, it brings its own particular powers to bear.* Let us look at just two of these particular powers.

Sonic simultaneity

A feature of most of the music we hear is that it combines two or more tones. Certainly, much music in history has not mixed its tones – Gregorian plainsong, for example. Nevertheless, the majority of music we encounter in the West today involves at least two tones being sung or played at once. An obvious feature of the perception of two sounds is that they do not occupy bounded zones in our aural field. Unlike two colours, which cannot be visible in the same space *as* two colours (one hides the other, or else they merge), sounds can be heard in and through each other while remaining perceptually distinct. Two notes fill the same heard 'space', yet we can hear them *as* two notes. They need not hide each other, nor merge. Composers have exploited this simple feature of sound perception to a remarkable degree, and in '*Kommt, ihr Töchter*' Bach does so in a myriad of ways to unfold an exceptionally rich theological vision. The chorus is a funeral procession in E minor for a multitude on their way to Jerusalem. And as the words will soon make clear, it also alludes to Jesus carrying his cross – indeed, his journey to Golgotha forms the central momentum of the *Passion*. A sense of heavy distress and undertow is evoked. A repeated note, a thudding pedal-point E is played on the lowest string of the basses. (There are forty of these notes before they start rising – Bach almost certainly had in mind the biblical symbolism of that number.) The leading upper melodies also begin on E but soon split, one tugging upward and the other downward, the two held in tension by the steadily pulsating bass Es. This three-fold texture generates an immediate sense of strain, the same process being repeated straight away at a higher pitch. The strain is intensified by a number of other devices, also involving overlapping tones. The upper melodies create and are interwoven with an extraordinary succession of chords, with frequent 'suspended dissonances' (when a line of melody is held over a change of harmony underneath, producing an acute tension). Especially pervasive is the 'tritone' (or augmented fourth), an interval with a long history in Western music, usually regarded as highly dissonant (dubbed by some medieval musicians the *diabolus in musica*) and associated with strife, precariousness and instability. In short, these carefully crafted superimpositions give rise to a multitude of tensions, and the fact that many of them are slow to resolve, and create further tensions, gives rise to an extraordinary impression of relentless driving against considerable opposition. The appropriateness of this need hardly be pointed out. Into this highly charged atmosphere, a choir enters. This is the daughter of Zion calling out to the faithful to behold the figure of Christ.[31] 'Come, you daughters, help me lament. Behold!' The faithful, on their way to Jerusalem, respond. This is a second choir – apprehensive believers, vaguely aware of impending catastrophe but baffled by this suffering figure. A dialogue ensues:

'Come, you daughters, help me lament. Behold ! '
'Whom?'
'The Bridegroom. Behold him !'
'How?'
'Like a lamb.'

Over this a third, heavenly choir (the '*ripieno*') sings a chorale, a metrical paraphrase of the *Agnus Dei* which concluded the Good Friday morning *Hauptgottesdienst*, the last line echoing the litany ('Have mercy on us, O Jesus'). The key is G major, the key of innocence in this *Passion*, here contrasting with the underlying key of E minor, the key of guilt.[32] This contrast between our guilt and the guiltless One who comes to bear our guilt away is in many ways the abiding theme of the work: the one possessing G major innocence was immersed in E minor tonality, for our sakes. And this music surrounds the silent figure on his way to Golgotha – in the manner of the Book of Revelation we witness a particular and unrepeatable death in Jerusalem and its eschatological significance from the perspective of the heavenly choir. The overlapping goes further still. The bass articulates the 'pastorale' rhythm, associated at this period (and in much music since) with shepherds and sheep. We recall that the *Agnus Dei* would have been sung earlier in the morning service; here the curtain is being drawn back upon the Lamb of God. The rhythm is trochaic, often employed in poetry to convey mystery, apprehension and anticipation. It is overlaid with the steady iambic rhythm of the chorale, a rhythm associated with stability, in this case, the bedrock of faith.[33] These are aligned skilfully and ironically – in the One trudging to his death, identifying with the apprehensive pilgrims, reliable salvation is being worked out.[34]

Waves of tension and resolution

Along with sonic simultaneity, we can draw attention to a second 'sacramental' capacity of musical sounds at work here. Bach's *Passions* stand in the tradition of 'Western tonal music', a tradition that now largely pervades music in the West (and beyond). It generally operates according to teleological principles: it is sensed as directional, we sense 'it is going somewhere'. This is produced primarily through the twin elements of tension and resolution. Sounds are created which, it is felt, cannot be left permanently as they are – they must be resolved in some manner, at some time. One of the ways in which this works out is through *metre*, music's basic beat-patterns. In '*Kommt, ihr Töchter*' metre is indicated by a 'time signature' (12/8). Here, there are four groups of three metrical beats. Of the three beats, the first is strong, the second weak, and the third 'leans' forward on to the strong first beat of the next three – generating a wave of tension and resolution, repeated over and over again.

But this process works on more than one level. The first beats of each of these waves are not of the same strength, and this generates another succession of waves 'higher up'. The first beats of those waves are also of different strength, generating yet another wave. And so on.

What emerges, then, is not a linear temporality but a multi-levelled momentum of tension and resolution, in which resolution at one level pushes forward a wave at another higher level. *One level's return is always another's advance.* Every return closes *and* opens, completes *and* extends, resolves *and* intensifies. Elsewhere, I have drawn out the remarkable resonances between this and patterns of promise and fulfilment, longing and resolving, stress and rest that pervade biblical faith.[35] Especially noteworthy is the way that in the Christian Scriptures, fulfilments of promises do not lessen hope, but intensify and augment it on another level – precisely the momentum we have just uncovered. In the *St Matthew Passion*, this many-layered dynamic could hardly be a more fitting vehicle for enabling a congregation to participate in some of the most pervasive features of the drama being unfolded – one only need think of the interplay of tension and resolution in the Passion text itself, the pervasiveness of the dynamics of promise and fulfilment, the continual maintenance of a 'not yet' which at the same time 'holds' people 'in the story', and so forth. All these could be explored through countless examples from this opening chorus alone.

Conclusion and postscript

In conclusion, let us step back a little. What have we learned from Bach? The upshot of our discussion of Blackwell was that if we are to use the discourse of sacrament and sacramentality to speak of the material mediation of divine reality, this should be done within a theological environment that pays due attention to the manner and distinctiveness of the free, gracious initiative of the triune God, climaxing in the life, death and resurrection of Jesus Christ (*the* sacrament), a God who is less a presence to discern than one who invites us into personal union and communion. One of the reasons we have chosen this Bach piece is because it so clearly inhabits such a theological environment – certainly in its original conception – and is thus especially apt for bringing to light the ways in which music may play a 'sacramental' role. The piece has the added advantage of being written before the concert hall aesthetic flourished, and thus can help us evade some of the difficulties that come with assuming that aesthetic to be normative – it is clear that this music's 'sacramental' power in Bach's day could not be abstracted from specific practices, nor from other media.[36] In this *Passion*, the most theologically important associated medium is words – the words of the biblical text and a carefully crafted commentary on that text. We discovered that *music, as it interacts with words, brings its own particular powers to bear*, and we examined ways in which two of music's particular powers contribute to the 'sacramental potential' of this piece.

This provokes a final reflection. Is this not one of those instances where we find that not only can theology serve music but music can serve theology, and not only serve a theology of 'sacramentality' as widely conceived but a theology of Baptism and Eucharist in particular? For what we have found surely has much to tell us about the vexed issue of the *relation between sacrament and word*, more precisely, about the relation between the material media of Baptism and Eucharist on the one hand, and Gospel words – read and preached – on the other. To reiterate: music, as it interacts with words, brings its own particular powers to bear. Let us take each side of that: (a) A material medium – musical sound – is combined with words in such a way that it does not simply ape the words in one-to-one correspondence, but interacts with them, *granting the hearer an intensely rich way of being drawn into the dynamic realities of which the words speak and in which the words are caught up.*[37] Music bears upon words and vice versa, generating possibilities greater than the sum of each; (b) In this interaction, *the particular properties and capacities of the material medium play a constitutive role.*[38] In '*Kommt, ihr Töchter*', there is undoubtedly a certain verbal primacy – the homiletic environment I have spoken about, grounded in Scripture – but we have seen enough to suggest that music *in its own ways* can bear witness to and mediate the momentum of triune grace to which those words direct us and in which the words are given to share.

Does Bach not model here the shape of a word–sacrament relation which (many would argue) comes close to that being evoked by the biblical material on Baptism and Eucharist and which many theologians have striven to articulate? Might not a close study of the word–music interaction in this and other pieces have much to tell us about fruitful (and unfruitful) ways of construing the word–sacrament interaction? Is not the way musical sounds appear to be operating here just the way in which the material media of Eucharist and Baptism are properly thought to be operating, interacting with the word while bringing their own particular capacities to bear? In the next ecumenical tussle about the relation of word and sacrament, might Bach have a place at the table?

187

Notes

1 Albert Blackwell, *The Sacred in Music* (Cambridge: Lutterworth, 1999).
2 Ibid., p. 28: quoting Richard McBrien.
3 For fuller treatments of this tradition, cf. Jamie James, *The Music of the Spheres: Music, Science and the Natural Order of the Universe* (London: Abacus, 1993); Giuseppe Massera, *Severino Boezio e la scienza armonica tra l'antichità e il Medio Evo* (Parma: Studium Parmense, 1976); M. L. West, *Ancient Greek Music* (Oxford: Clarendon, 1992).
4 Blackwell, *The Sacred in Music*, p. 69.
5 Ibid., pp. 56ff.
6 Ibid., pp. 80ff. He calls this 'propaedeutics – "pre-commitment" preparation for beliefs', p. 82.
7 Ibid., p. 99.
8 Ibid., pp. 133ff.
9 Ibid., p. 159.
10 Ibid., pp. 167f.
11 Ibid., p. 84.
12 Cf. Daniel Chua, *Absolute Music and the Construction of Meaning* (Cambridge: Cambridge University Press, 1999), ch. 3. Blackwell's response to one of the discrepancies highlights the difficulties: the acoustic anomaly known as the 'Pythagorean comma' – the Pythagorean interval of a 5th, if repeated upwards (or downwards) will not lead one back to the note from which one started, but to one very close by. Blackwell speaks of this as representing a 'fundamental flaw in the orderly structure of the musical cosmos' (Blackwell, *The Sacred in Music*, p. 156), 'analogous' to the presence of temptation and sin, evil and suffering. But why, we might ask, should the Pythagorean comma be regarded as a *dis*order? The problem here seems to be an over-keenness to give divine sanction to a particular type of mathematical order. (Ironically, he seems at one stage to give this very disorder some kind of divine status, directly intended – for he claims that God has 'set up the musical cosmos' in this 'inherently discordant' way. Is he claiming the same of evil and suffering?)

13 For fuller discussion, cf. Jeremy Begbie, *Theology, Music and Time* (Cambridge: Cambridge University Press, 2000), pp. 276ff. Also Colin Gunton, *The Triune Creator: A Historical and Systematic Study* (Edinburgh: Edinburgh University Press, 1998), pp. 111ff.

14 See Wolterstorff's discussion of 'sign-agency conceptuality' and 'God-agency conceptuality', in Nicholas Wolterstorff, 'Sacrament as Action not Presence', in David Brown and Ann Loades (eds), *Christ: the Sacramental Word* (London: SPCK, 1996), pp. 103–22.

15 See Begbie, *Theology, Music and Time*. Cf. Rowan Williams, 'The Nature of a Sacrament', in *On Christian Theology* (Oxford: Blackwell, 2001), p. 201.

16 He writes: 'I am in my fashion a trinitarian, believing that whatever we mean by God, the concepts applied must be dynamic, whole, and commodious, relational, mutual, and stable, such as triangularity is well suited to symbolize'. (Blackwell, *The Sacred in Music*, p. 18).

17 Cf. Williams, 'The Nature of a Sacrament', p. 197.

18 Cf. Blackwell, *The Sacred in Music*, pp. 15ff.

19 Nicholas Wolterstorff, 'The Work of Making a Work of Music', in P. J. Alperson (ed.), *What is Music? An Introduction to the Philosophy of Music* (University Park: Pennsylvania State University Press, 1987), pp. 127, 128.

20 Wolterstorff, 'The Work of Making a Work of Music', p. 128.

21 The literature is vast, but cf., for example, Nicholas Cook and Mark Everest (eds), *Rethinking Music* (Oxford: Oxford University Press, 1999); Tia DeNora, *Music in Everyday Life* (Cambridge: Cambridge University Press, 2000); Nicholas Cook, *Music: A Very Short Introduction* (Oxford: Oxford University Press, 1998).

22 DeNora, *Music in Everyday Life*, p. ix.

23 For a very persuasive treatment of this, cf. John Cook, *Analysing Musical Multimedia* (Oxford: Clarendon Press, 1998).

24 There is no need to assume that the performance of this piece today must attempt to replicate the conditions of the first performance (or some ideal setting Bach may have had in mind) in order to be 'sacramental'.

25 Robin A. Leaver, 'The Mature Vocal Works and Their Theological and Liturgical Context', in John Butt (ed.), *The Cambridge*

Companion to Bach (Cambridge: Cambridge University Press, 1997), p. 107.

26 Bach's librettist was Picander (Christian Friedrich Henrici), a poet responsible for a large number of occasional sacred texts, many of which Bach used in his cantatas. With its mixture of Gospel text and complex madrigal-style poetry, Picander's *St Matthew Passion* libretto enabled Bach to compose a wholly original work in a single sweep.

27 The service would begin with an opening hymn for the congregation – most probably *'Da Jesus an dem Kreuze stund'* ('Our blessed Saviour seven times spoke' – a hymn on the seven last words from the cross). It would end, after the Passion setting, with the Good Friday collect, followed by the hymn *'Nun danket alle Gott'* ('Now thank we all our God'). (See Robin A. Leaver, *Music as Preaching: Bach, Passions and Music in Worship* (Oxford: Latimer Press, 1982).)

28 As Leaver shows, the five elements traditionally attributed to a sermon by Lutheran theologians can all be found in Bach's *Passions*. (*Music as Preaching*, pp. 21–7.) Cf. also W. Böhme (ed.), *Johann Sebastian Prediger in Tönen* (Karlsruhe: Evangelische Akademie, 1985).

29 This corresponds to the *'Applicatio'* in the Lutheran sermon: evoking a response from the congregation, something done principally in the chorales of the Passions. Cf. *Music as Preaching*, pp. 22f.

30 Eric Chafe, *Tonal Allegory in the Vocal Music of J. S. Bach* (Berkeley, CA: University of California Press, 1991), pp. 337ff. ('The *St Matthew Passion*: The Lutheran Meditative Tradition').

31 The 'daughter of Zion' is a complex figure in the *St Matthew Passion*. Bach and Picander combine her prophetic and priestly role with her allegorical representation as the New Jerusalem. Cf. Edward Savage, 'The *St. Matthew Passion* as a Drama of Conversion', *Church Music* (1980), p. 80, 58f.

32 *Tonal Allegory*, pp. 368ff. Strictly speaking, this is not superimposition (G major sung directly over E minor), but the two keys are nevertheless in immediate juxtaposition.

33 'The *St. Matthew Passion* as a Drama of Conversion', pp. 57f.

34 I explore the theological significance of musical simultaneity

further in Jeremy S. Begbie (ed.), *Beholding the Glory: Incarnation through the Arts* (London: Darton, Longman & Todd, 2000), ch. 8.

35 See Begbie, *Theology, Music and Time*, esp. chs. 2 and 4.

36 Ironically, it was quickly subsumed into that milieu (as a 'great' concert work). It is significant that Mendelssohn's famous performance in 1829, which introduced the piece to the modern concert-going public, took place not in a church but in the hall of the Berlin *Singakademie*.

37 Too often the music-word relation has been theorized according to a spectrum running from strict conformance to outright conflict, the former usually being held up as the ideal. But, as Nicholas Cook has recently contended, music *interacts* with other media in mutual interplay. (Cook, *Analysing Musical Multimedia*, chs. 2 and 3.)

38 In fact, Bach is even more instructive in this respect than we have indicated. He was composing at a critical time in the European tradition when the ancient Pythagorean tradition was waning, when music was increasingly distanced from any divine ordering of the world and frequently tied to the order of word. Bach knew these verbally-oriented traditions well, but it would seem that he had substantial sympathy with movements in Lutheranism and beyond which insisted that music is, more fundamentally, a negotiation and exploration of the rich God-given order of the cosmos. Cf., for example, Robert L. Marshall, 'Truth and Beauty: J. S. Bach at the Crossroads of Cultural History', in Paul Brainard and Ray Robinson (eds), *A Bach Tribute: Essays in Honor of William H. Scheide* (Chapel Hill, NC: Hinshaw, 2000), pp. 179–188.

Index